THE LONG ROAD TO JUSTICE

THE LONG ROAD
TO JUSTICE

UNRAVELING ALEX MURDAUGH'S TANGLED WEB

JUROR 864 AMIE WILLIAMS
with Shana Hirsch

PALMETTO
PUBLISHING
Charleston, SC
www.PalmettoPublishing.com

Hardcover ISBN: 9798822954212
Paperback ISBN: 9798822954229

"A court is no better than each of you sitting before me on this jury. A court is only as sound as its jury, and a jury is only as sound as the men who make it up."
– Atticus Finch (*To Kill a Mockingbird*)

For: My Fellow Jurors & the victims of Domestic Violence and their children who will benefit from the services provided at Sanctuary House: Healing Hearts & Changing Lives

"You're not a victim for sharing your story. You are a survivor setting the world on fire with your truth. And you never know who needs your light, your warmth and raging courage."
– Alex Elle

For: The Branstetter and Proctor Families and the countless others once trapped in Alex Murdaugh's tangled web

"A truthful and personal account that captures the reader from the start and engages them throughout its entirety. For those from the surrounding area and those fascinated by true crime, the writer's personality and wit permeate every page. It's a perspective that is rarely shared."

— Elizabeth Dardes, editor of *The Long Road to Justice: Unravelling Alex Murdaugh's Tangled Web*

"Buckle your seatbelts for a front-row seat to the Alex Murdaugh trial. Amie Williams and Shana Hirsch take the reader on the turbulent experience of being a juror in one of the most high-profile criminal cases the Lowcountry has seen. Amie walks you through an experience that feels relatable. Her observations, thoughts, fears, and, most importantly, her vantage, point of being up close and personal with the case and the man himself, Alex Murdaugh. *The Long Road to Justice: Unravelling Alex Murdaugh's Tangled Web* hits all the textures and nuances of Amie's experience and is a book you are not going to want to miss."

— Paul, host of the YouTube channel *Reporting Live from My Sofa.*

"Experience what it is like to sit in the jury box during one of the most notorious legal events of the century. Fascinating and well written, *The Long Road to Justice: Unravelling Alex Murdaugh's Tangled Web* is a must read for those who followed the case in the trial of Alex Murdaugh."

– Kim Poovey, bestselling author of *Shadows of the War.*

"The Gordons are kindred spirits with Juror 864 Amie Williams and co-writer Shana Hirsch. We are all authors who peeled back layers of the Murdaugh onion and after many tears—endured to write about it. Their book *The Long Road to Justice: Unravelling Alex Murdaugh's Tangled Web* transports the reader into the jury box before, during, and after South Carolina's trial of the century. We started reading it one Saturday and never put it down!"

– Neil and Melissa Gordon, www.trialwatchers.com

TABLE OF CONTENTS

AUTHOR'S NOTE

I shed my anonymity as Juror 864 the second I walked on the set of *Today* for our jury interview with Craig Melvin. Immediately after that aired, I was surprised my phone did not short circuit from the barrage of incoming text messages and emails from friends and family saying, "I did not know you were on the jury." You, dear reader, have probably chosen my story because, like millions, you did not miss a day of trial coverage and likely stayed up way too late watching legal analysis on YouTube. That is not a criticism. If not for avid, curious trial watchers demanding truth and justice, I may not have been led to my co-author.

We met through a colleague of mine. When I finally returned to work, he said, "I have a friend who obsessed over the trial every day. She wanted me to tell you, 'Thank you;' and she wants to take you to dinner because she has questions. Oh, and she'll write your book!" I began to think, if the people I know had a million questions, what about the ones I don't know? In the months following the verdict, I prayed over the idea of sharing my experience. Then one day I realized I had an interesting story to tell and an audience who wanted (hopefully) to hear it. So, I called Shana and said, "Were you serious when you said you'd write my story? If so, I need an author." Thankfully, her shriek of excitement when accepting my offer did not cause permanent hearing damage. We officially kicked off our author/co-author era in July (2023).

When we first sat down to brainstorm ideas, it did not take either one of us very long to realize that she had a base of trial knowledge that was non-existent to me (and my fellow jurors, for that matter). Remember, she watched it gavel-to-gavel on Court TV, so if the cameras were rolling, she was glued to coverage, while we were in the jury room. One such example, is when Shana bought me a coffee mug that read, "Bring the Jury." She said, "As I was gift wrapping that, it dawned on me you have absolutely no idea that was what Judge Newman said to the bailiff when he was ready for y'all to enter the courtroom." We decided the best way to have the most streamlined point-of-view would be for me to rewatch the trial. This ended up being a good plan of attack, especially when writing on specific witnesses and testimony.

It is of paramount importance that my readers first trust me as a juror—who strictly adhered to her oath—and secondly as a narrator. In early drafts we had declarative statements like "in my post-verdict research" as signal phrases to set up expert quotations. We both thought it was far too repetitive and hindered the narrative's flow.

So, as we travel down this long road to justice together, I ask that you please remember, **_any and all_** research on SC vs. Richard

Alexander Murdaugh did not commence until July of 2023, when Shana first put pen to paper and began *The Long Road to Justice*: *Unraveling Alex Murdaugh's Tangled Web*. We hope you enjoy the journey as much as we did, bringing it to life.

PREFACE:
HAVE MERCY JUDGE

Approximately 32 million jury summonses are sent in the United States each year. Despite being a prospective juror for what local news was calling the trial of the century, I did not burst into song or do a happy dance when my summons arrived. Nor did I think to fabricate an elaborate story in hopes of being excused. I simply reasoned that the probability of me ending up on the jury was quite low, as a reported 900 summons were mailed and only 18 seats would be filled. Spoiler alert, you're reading my memoir, so obviously the odds were not in my favor. After only two and a half days of jury selection, the twelve of us and six alternates took our oath.

Once I received my summons, it would be about six weeks before I had to report for jury selection at the Colleton County Courthouse. During this time, we were instructed to avoid watching and reading the news. I am assuming this was due, in part, to the rampant media coverage associated with the case itself and the mounting charges that kept Alex Murdaugh a top story across countless news outlets. This meant I would be enjoying my dinner while watching *NCIS*, *CSI*, or *Law and Order*, rather than the nightly news. For all the unpredictability that exists in the world, there is one certainty, a marathon of these popular police procedurals is always available somewhere.

With the upcoming trial on my mind, it was difficult not to pay attention to what was happening in the jury box. Did they appear engaged? Did they cry when witnesses gave powerful testimony? Did they recoil in horror when learning graphic details about the crime?

Don't worry, the guilty vote I returned had nothing to do with my television viewing habits. However, what Tinseltown fails to acknowledge is the tremendous emotional burden carried by jurors, especially in criminal cases, as a guilty verdict will carry a lifetime (or two in Alex's case) of consequences. There is an indescribable heft that comes with being 1/12 of a singular body charged with determining the guilt or innocence of another human being.

I believe having a historical and cultural awareness of our jury system will offer a framework for this judicial life force and garner appreciation for the responsibilities shouldered by jurors world-wide every day. The introduction which follows is comprised of the four sections summarized below. It is meant to act as a foundational roadmap for your journey down the long and winding road to justice.

I. **Pop Culture**: Movies, television, and reels (short videos) saturate our daily lives. Although there is no mandate on accuracy, we often turn to them as a guide for informing the unknown.

II. **Historical Context**: This section provides a succinct history of the jury system.

III. **Jury Duty: a loathed mandate**: I explore some reasons behind America's sweeping view of this civic duty as an annoyance and inconvenience.

IV. **The Colleton County Courthouse**: For almost a century, the Murdaugh family had a stranglehold over the Fourteenth Judicial Circuit, so I felt a brief history would provide context for our history-making verdict.

After my six weeks of jury service concluded, colleagues, friends, and strangers (friends of friends) had a lot of questions. If my phone was not blowing up with text messages, my email's inbox would overflow. Quickly I realized there was a large, captive audience genuinely interested in hearing about my experience as Juror 864 for Alex Murdaugh's double murder trial. Despite my initial feelings of overwhelm, I put pen to paper, soon intelligible words started filling the page and a book began to develop.

One of the first things people are curious to know is if we were allowed to take notes during the trial, and the answer is "No." We were given notebooks which stayed in our respective jury room. On breaks, Judge Newman encouraged us to jot down any questions we may want to discuss in *deliberation*. At the conclusion of each day, they were secured in the courthouse.

You may recall during opening statements, Creighton Waters discussed the complicated nature of the case but reassured us his team was working hard to ensure there would be little room for confusion when the prosecution rested its case. They did just that, for we had very few questions among us. I share this anecdote to reemphasize that my decision to author a book came months after my civic duty concluded. It was not anything I considered while sitting in the jury box. Day-after-day, exhibit-after-exhibit, and testimony-after-testimony, I listened attentively. My only goal was to understand this multifaceted case and to return a verdict consistent with the evidence presented throughout the six weeks of trial.

My primary goal was to tell a story which both would "please and instruct" by sharing tales of challenges and levity from within the jury box to the jury room(s) along the backdrop of scholarly analysis. From the forward through the afterward, I anticipate you will feel like a thirteenth juror as we reexamine the key components which led to our unanimous guilty verdict.

INTRODUCTION:
TEAR IT UP AND
THROW IT AWAY

I: THE JURY'S ROLE IN POP CULTURE

The double-murder trial of Alex Murdaugh attracted an audience of millions across the globe. With such a tremendous viewership, it is reasonable to assume that not everyone has served on a jury, which is the principal reason I am beginning my story with a discussion of Hollywood courtrooms and their potential impact on jurors.

Television's *Perry Mason* began the "courtroom procedural" and provided Hollywood a gold-standard that is still thriving today, even undergoing a reboot in 2020. Speaking to its timeless impact, Ron Fitzgerald (a creator and executive producer of the remake) stated, "*Perry Mason* is the show that launched a thousand shows; every courtroom drama you've ever seen comes from that template." For example, each week *Law and Order* viewers eagerly anticipate a verdict from the twelve non-speaking extras in the jury box. Film and media scholar Carol Clover refers to this depiction as either a "passive jury" or "human furniture." They are not portrayed as individuals moving in the courthouse, deliberating, or doing the work of actual jurors. Another function of this "passive jury" is to serve as a captive audience for a leading actor's impassioned monologue, as seen in *To Kill a Mockingbird* (1967) and *The Verdict* (1982), for example.

Although nearly two decades separate the films, the attorneys command the lead as they work to expose a two-tiered system of justice. Lastly, failing to mention the legal thriller pioneer, John Grisham, would just be negligent. Even the most zealous fan cannot argue his steady use of the passive jury, save for *Runaway Jury* (2003). Speaking of Grisham, he was never in attendance at the trial of the century. The doppelgänger who set social media ablaze for an afternoon was the mayor of Walterboro, William T. Young.

Conversely, there are rare instances where the jury takes center stage, as in the drama *12 Angry Men* (1957), while the zany Pauly Shore taught us the exact wrong way to be a good juror in the outlandish comedy *Jury Duty* (1995). Most recently the streaming service Freevee launched an eight-episode series called *Jury Duty* (2023) which can be described as, "a mockumentary that turns an everyday American experience into a hilarious reality TV experiment as it explores the progression of a civil trial in California through the eyes of one juror who does not realize that everyone, except him, is an actor."

Fear not, I did not study for my summons by analyzing television and movies. However, it cannot be disputed that courtrooms, both fictional and real-life, dominate the entertainment industry making it almost impossible not to consider its potential influence on the jury system.

Scholar David Papke explains the correlation, "Pop culture prompts, encourages, and refines views of social reality and has the potential to affect how generic devotees see their world."[6] In summary, average consumers of courtroom dramas may have a skewed perception of the responsibility that comes with serving on a jury. It is likely this was on the minds of both the prosecution and defense, as they queried our television habits prior to jury selection. Likewise, Judge Patricia Marks expressed a similar concern when she saw a post from a potential juror who said he was preparing for his civic duty by watching jury-centered films.

II: HISTORY OF THE JURY SYSTEM

To fully appreciate the immeasurable responsibility which comes with serving on a jury, I want to provide a brief historical framework for context. *Most* people, myself included, who are not part of the legal community, have a fundamental understanding of the judicial system which can likely be summed up in 3 key phrases: "12 ordinary citizens," "a jury of your peers," and "civic duty."

The United States jury system finds its roots in ancient Greece where it was comprised exclusively of males over 30. Greeks held the steadfast belief that "jury trials were the best way to ensure that the community's sense of justice would prevail, rather than just the beliefs or leanings of one person." Aristotle further emphasized these *men* were told to refrain from interpreting the law and instructed to *apply* their "understanding of 'general justice.'"

Our jury system mirrors this ancient belief but with modern adaptations like age and gender requisites. This legal structure was so impressive many foreign counterparts looked toward the American courtroom as their judicial prototype. French aristocrat Alexis de Tocqueville felt "the community's collective wisdom was the best judge of the actions of others because only a government that trusts the people's judgment can support an impartial system." Centuries later in *South Carolina vs. Alex Murdaugh,* de Tocqueville's sentiment would speak to the heart of a key argument made by the state. The people's trust in Alex was broken which was reflective of the larger, shattered system which dominated the Fourteenth Judicial Circuit for nearly a century. For the first time in Alex Murdaugh's life, he was being held to account for his actions.

III. WHY DO PEOPLE LOATH JURY DUTY?

To most people, jury service is a governmental obligation that, with any kind of luck, can sometimes be avoided. Stanley from sitcom's *The Office* is the rare exception of someone who longed for a summons stating, "I have been trying to get on jury duty every single year since I was 18 years old. To get to sit in an air-conditioned room downtown, judging people while my lunch was paid for? That is the life!" Research shows, however, there are very few Stanleys.

Among the millions who are sent summonses each year, with dread, rather than elation being their pervading feeling, as shown in "A Juror's Prayer:"

Dear God, please give me an excuse in a hurry,
Something good to keep me off this stupid jury.
My job! My kids! My sick Aunt Bea!
Who could survive even a day without me?
And you should know, by the way, I'm deaf in one ear,
So when a witness testifies, I won't be able to hear.
Here comes the defense lawyer, eyes right on me.
"Just because my client's been charged, do you think he's guilty?"
"Actually, I do," I say, trying hard not to smirk.
"If not of this crime, then because he's a jerk!"
But be warned, Mr. State Attorney, don't think I'll help you,
You see, I hate the police, informants, and prosecutors, too!
Now is the time, the *voir dire est fini,*
Please, God, don't let them pick me.
Did I mention I'm scheduled for brain surgery?

This humorous poem illustrates the ennui felt among Americans when they see that little envelope in their mailbox. While it may seem like the poem is over-the-top, *The New York Post*'s article, "The Wackiest Excuses People use to get out of Jury Duty" shows just how much truth there can be in satire, such convoluted stories include:

5

- Alan Dershowitz recalled this story: When one of my books came out about how I defend people, someone on a jury in the Southern District of Manhattan was kicked off for carrying it. The book was 1982's *The Best Defense*, which 'talked a lot about the presumption of innocence' and was critical of prosecutors. 'Word got around, and a whole bunch of people came in carrying my book. I think that's what made my book a best-seller.'

- What you wear to court could perhaps get you kicked out of the jury pool. James Lowe, of Barnet, Vermont, showed up decked out in a black-and white-striped prisoner jumpsuit, complete with matching beanie and was dismissed from jury duty.

I consider myself to be creative, clever, and even courageous but these courtroom hijinks are a tour de force. Conversely, the research also shows very real and relatable reasons for not wanting to fulfill this civic duty. A 2021 study surveyed 1,184 individuals who had either received a summons or served on a jury. The results indicated nearly 10% fibbed to evade jury duty, citing "reasons" such as unmitigated bias, medical issues, or travel plans. Despite the obvious lies they told, their reasons were legitimate with an overarching economic theme, "48.2% stated it was a financial inconvenience; 19.3% feared consequences from their employer, and 15.7% lacked access to childcare for the trial's duration." These are true-to-life concerns which warrant further study and proposed solutions, especially in the instance of a lengthy criminal trial.

Economic consequences are a paramount concern for potential jurors all over the United States. However, for many of those in Colleton County, their unease, financial or otherwise, was compounded by innate fear. South Carolina attorney Eric Bland stated, "Although the legal dynasty seemed to be crumbling more and more daily, people remained scared of the Murdaughs because after all, 'they were the law.'" Potential jurors were calling him very nervous that they were going to get selected. Being a resident of Colleton County, I had certainly heard tales of this and am grateful to never have experienced it firsthand.

IV: COLLETON COUNTY COURTHOUSE

There were many extraordinary variables at play for this trial of the century. For one, it was held in the Colleton County Courthouse where four generations of Murdaughs had tried countless cases. This added a level of intrigue for locals, residents throughout the five counties which comprise the Fourteenth Judicial Circuit, and knowledgeable trial watchers. While the location may seem trifling to some, it most certainly was not.

For almost a century, the Murdaughs wielded an unbelievable amount of power and influence across the state. So much so, a portrait of Alex's grandfather hangs in the very courtroom where we sat in judgement of his grandson, an accused family annihilator. To ensure a fair trial, Judge Newman ordered its temporary removal. The portrait, or rather its absence, both began and ended the trial, as Judge Newman referenced it again at sentencing.

It is my hope this discussion, along with my evidentiary memoir, will reassure family members, victims, trial watchers, and even the skeptics, that we, the jury, returned a result consistent with witness testimony and the presented evidence. It was our job to seek the truth and be a voice for Maggie and Paul. Without a modicum of fear among us, we delivered our true verdict, thereby upholding the immortal words of Dr. Martin King, Jr. "Injustice anywhere is a threat to justice everywhere."

FOREWORD:
WATCHING THE DETECTIVES

By: Dr. Kenny Kinsey

On Monday June 7, 2021, Alex Murdaugh stood in the drizzling Lowcountry rain with cell phone in hand. As Murdaugh spoke to a law enforcement dispatcher, he uttered the words, "My wife and child have been shot badly." Absent divine intervention, one could never imagine the impact that those eight words would have on the conscious of thousands, both in and around the otherwise quiet rural surroundings. Families would be changed forever. A wife, mother, sister, aunt, and friend lay deceased on the wet grass nearby. In close proximity, a loved but troubled son and brother was immediately no more. A generational dynasty would forevermore be altered. A dynasty that history had shown to be both envied and feared by some, while utilized or avoided by others.

The thirteen months following the murders of Maggie and Paul Murdaugh would create speculation and theories amongst most. Those with personal knowledge of the deeds, both good and bad of the legacy called Murdaugh would stay constantly connected to the ever-changing story of what took place at Moselle, and what transpired prior to the events that could produce such an outcome. Would the killer or killers ever be discovered? Would law enforcement get that much needed lucky break? Would the Murdaugh family get their pound of justice? Could the memories of Maggie and Paul ever be associated with happier times? These are the questions that fueled the many talented investigators that undertook this challenge.

The tragedy would finally culminate in the picturesque town of Walterboro, South Carolina. There, the media would introduce the entire world to both entanglement and southern hospitality, in the backdrop of the local courthouse, rich with historical significance. A battle would be fought there in real-time. This battle would prove to be a legal reckoning, unlike anything ever encountered by most. Unlike the battles of the 1860s, there were no sabers or muskets. There was no marching or protests like witnessed in the civil rights struggles of the 1950s and 1960s. No looting or rioting occurred like seen in the 1990s in another famous trial on an opposite coast, but a battle of wits between savvy high dollar defense attorneys, who were worthy of their price, and skilled career prosecutors with over a combined century of experience at representing victims.

This book, *The Long Road to Justice: Unraveling Alex Murdaugh's Tangled Web* is about a group of diverse individuals who answered their call to civic duty, and the perspective as lived by one of those civic minded jury members. Despite putting her life on hold, she along with other members sacrificed family, occupation, and has managed the extreme juror-stress that is carried post-verdict. Although in complete control of the proceedings, "Your Honor" is technically the referee. Tasked with much more responsibility than calling balls and strikes, but with maintaining order and decorum, and providing the sole and final instruction of the law. The deliberated verdict of a jury should always be commended, accepted, and never faulted, for they are the real judges of credibility and fact.

Despite the biblical penalty for breaking the laws of God, Earthly consequences also exist. Murder is the most severe crime that is committed against Man's law. The frequency of our heinous actions, and the methods that are often utilized seem unfathomable to many. Failure to understand the threshold for guilt, and our adversarial system has been known to divide family and friends. It really doesn't matter what we think, those men and women who step forward with a willingness to do society's bidding should be understood.

Thank you to the members of this jury for your sacrifice. Some will never understand what you experienced but I do. God bless the memory of Maggie and Paul.

God bless us all, Dr. Kinsey

PART I

"We learned about honesty and integrity—that truth matters, that you don't take shortcuts or play by your own set of rules, and that success doesn't count unless you earn it fair and square."

—Michelle Obama

CHAPTER 1:
RETURN TO SENDER

Over lunch one day, a friend resentfully mentioned getting a jury summons. I sheepishly bowed my head to avoid eye contact and mumbled, "I have never even received a summons." She grimaced. Not wanting to jeopardize my good fortune, I knocked on the nearest piece of wood. Well, what soon followed either meant I knocked on laminate, or someone from the Colleton County Courthouse heard my confession. Regardless, once they launched their harassment campaign, a deluge of summonses soon littered my mailbox.

About six months after I jinxed myself, there it was, just lying among the Christmas catalogs—my first-ever summons. I called my friend lamenting that my lucky streak was broken. We shared a good laugh. Once the sting subsided, I became genuinely interested and was excited to do my civic duty.

After going through the entire qualification process, we were told the case was about sexual harassment. As a survivor, I felt there was no room for objectivity and asked to be dismissed. My request was granted. I took my leave, confident this effort would remove me from the pool, at least for a little while. I could not have been more wrong!

Not even a year later, I spied the Colleton County crest poking out among my bills and weekly circular. To be honest, this time, I considered calling in with a tale of woe. Perhaps "killing" off an uncle or feigning organ donation might sound plausible. I decided against being untruthful and showed up for the assigned date. This time I was chosen as one of the two alternates for a car accident case. The original jurors served throughout the week-long trial, so I was not part of the deliberation. Once the verdict was delivered, we were dismissed. I left the courthouse just knowing *this time* my name would be removed from the pool, for at least a minimum of two years.

Obviously, my *limited* capacity as an alternate was not enough to end Colleton County's relentless pursuit. In December 2022, a third summons found its way into my mailbox. This time, I shuddered. I could not figure out what in the world the Clerk of Court wanted with me this time. I have never heard of a "jury member of the year award," but maybe I was being chosen as their premier honoree. Surely it was not —it could not be—oh it was, a *third* summons.

As I opened the envelope, sighing, "Why me," something seemed different. There was a distinguishable thickness to this one which set it apart from the others. Inside was a lengthy questionnaire that read suspiciously like a dating profile. My curiosity was piqued. How did my bumper stickers, club affiliations, or favorite television shows impact my ability to decide a person's guilt or innocence? Looking over the cryptic survey, something felt

STATE OF SOUTH CAROLINA   **JUROR SUMMONS FOR CIRCUIT COURT**

COUNTY OF: Colleton   FOR TERM BEGINNING WEEK OF: 1/23/2023   JUROR NUMBER: 864

You are hereby summoned to appear at Colleton County Courthouse, 101 Hampton Street, Walterboro, SC 29488   on **1/23/2023 at 3:00:00 PM** to answer this summons to serve as a petit juror for the Court of Common Pleas and General Sessions. Failure to appear at the address above at the specified time may subject you to penalties as prescribed by law.

Clerk of Court, **Rebecca H. Hill**   Panel:JAN. 23, 2023 Phone: (843) 549-5791 x

NAME AND ADDRESS OF JUROR	IMPORTANT INFORMATION AND INSTRUCTIONS
WILLIAMS, AMIE S	Fill in the requested information in the "Juror Information Section" and the appropriate contact information below. After reading all the conditions listed in the "Juror Response Section," mark any condition that applies to you. Separate the top and bottom portions of this page at the line indicated below and WITHIN THREE DAYS OF RECEIPT return the bottom portion of the form using the self-addressed envelope provided.

NOTE: PERSONS FAILING TO RETURN THESE FORMS AS REQUESTED MAY BE SUBJECT TO CHARGES OF CONTEMPT OF COURT
Separate this top portion from bottom portion at the dotted line. Retain this top portion for your reference.

ATTENTION JURORS

Proper Dress is Required in the Courtroom!

The Judiciary requires appropriate attire in the courtroom, specifically; No shorts, tank tops, hats or inappropriate dress. NO CELL PHONES OR OTHER COMMUNICATION DEVICES will be allowed in the Courthouse.

If you have additional questions, you may contact Sherry Robinson, General Sessions Deputy Clerk OR Cindy Nettles in my office, by calling the following number: 843-549-5791(FOR QUESTIONS----ONLY)

PLEASE CALL 843-549-1775 ON FRIDAY, JANUARY 20, 2023 AFTER 6:00 P.M. FOR AN UPDATE MESSAGE REGARDING YOUR JURY SERVICE.

County Parking Lot on Jefferies Boulevard across from the Courthouse is available for parking.

Thank you for your respect of the Court System.
Rebecca H. Hill, Clerk of Court

eerily familiar about the date I was to report for jury selection, January 23rd. I reviewed my day planner; it was no one's birthday; I did not have a church function, and there was nothing out of the ordinary scheduled at work. I paused for a second, recalling an earlier news report that Alex Murdaugh waived his right, at the last minute, to appear at a pre-trial status hearing. Was I among the hundreds in that jury pool? My curiosity got the best of me, so I googled, "When does the Murdaugh trial begin?" My immediate reaction was total shock. I called my mom, screaming, "Mom, Mom, my summons is for the Murdaugh Trial!!" Laughing, she said, "Oh yeah."

State of South Carolina
The Circuit Court of the Third Judicial Circuit

December 9, 2022

Dear Prospective Juror:

You have been summoned to potentially serve as a juror in a criminal trial in the Court of General Sessions for Colleton County beginning **Monday, January 23, 2023.**

Jury duty is an extremely important civic duty for which you are not frequently called upon to perform. It requires your careful attention and devotion.

In every criminal trial it is essential that the verdict of a jury be based solely upon the evidence presented in court and the law which applies to the case. Prior to receiving this notice, you may have read, seen, or heard information relating to this case. From this point on, it is critical that you not allow yourself to be exposed to any type of media coverage. Discussions with family members, friends, potential jurors, or any other persons concerning any facts or circumstances related to this case is prohibited. Do not read newspaper articles, watch television, listen to the radio, or listen to any other news accounts or reports.

You are required to complete the enclosed questionnaire along with the Juror Information Card attached to your Summons and return it to the Clerk of Court in the enclosed envelope within **five (5) days of receipt.**

I look forward to seeing you on **Monday, January 23, 2023, at the Colleton County Courthouse, 101 Hampton Street, Walterboro, South Carolina.**

Sincerely,

Clifton Newman
Presiding Judge

Working my way through the questionnaire, I could not help but utter, "Here we go again." It was very tempting to provide absurd answers—the ones I suspected they did *not* want to hear. As usual, my conscience prevented the ruse, and I told the whole truth and nothing but the truth. I have two bumper stickers: 1) He > I and 2) GWU Parent (Gardner Webb University). I am active in my church. I don't watch true crime documentaries, but I enjoy police procedurals. People often ask if I ever tried to get out of serving on that jury. I always answer "No." However, what happened just after Labor Day weekend of 2023 made me wish I had never served. If I had any inkling Dick and Jim's names would still be in my mouth a year later, I would have taken a sledgehammer to my tried-and-true moral compass and fabricated an award-winning excuse. Having a crucial role in Dick and Jim's sideshow was not how I wanted to end last year and begin the new one.

I arrived at the Colleton County Courthouse bright and early that January morning for the first day of jury selection. Some folks fell into the list of exemptions set forth by Judge Newman which included, "not being able to miss work, had no arranged childcare or had recently served on other juries." Once the group had been winnowed down, Judge Newman asked those who remained "more specific questions about the case, like whether they had an opinion on Murdaugh's guilt or innocence, and whether they knew any of the case's potential witnesses."[1]

After making it through this initial qualification process, we were directed to report back Wednesday. On our second day, the entire pool had been culled to 120 potential jurors. Many of whom were reluctant to serve. Some people did not have to work too hard to be excused. One woman was employed at a local grocery store and worked in the deli. She was the sole employee responsible for preparing the breakfast buffet. Another was very determined not to be among the final 18 empaneled jurors. Over and over (and over), she presented valid reasons for excusal; however, none were powerful enough to stick. Nevertheless, she persisted and was finally granted the heave-ho on her fourth and final attempt when she said, "I work where the defense team is staying." The room erupted in laughter.

Destined to be among the final eighteen, I answered the questionnaire truthfully and did not create conflict when Judge Newman asked the pointed questions related to the case. I was there to serve if called upon because, as Abraham Lincoln reminds us, "the greatest service of citizenship is jury duty."

CHAPTER 2:
YOU'RE THE ONE THAT I WANT

The final stage of jury selection is *voir dire* which means "to speak the truth." In a typical South Carolina case, either the judge or lawyers ask questions of the entire panel. However, as I am sure you have gleaned from the saturation of media coverage, nothing is *ever* typical in Murdaugh World. For us, *voir dire* meant standing before the prosecution and defense, like show dogs at Westminster. There is no word or phrase in the English language which describes how it felt to be face-to-face with the black-eyed, hoary redhead.

Before it was my turn to walk on the courtroom runway, I watched the spectacle from my seat. Alex Murdaugh was in complete control of choosing *his* jury. I don't recall if I recognized this at the time, but looking back, it is very clear that Alex was choosing people that he felt could be easily manipulated.

Alex eyed us all head-to-toe. There seemed to be a smarmy twinkle in his eye each time he gave Dick and Jim his nod of approval to seat the juror—almost like he was doing us a favor. After yeeting many and seating eleven, it was my turn to take the stage. Alex smiled sickeningly at me and nodded "yes." There was something about this exchange that left me with a powerful feeling of unease. His gaze reminded me of a classic soap opera villain who stares longingly into the camera after finding the ideal patsy to carry out his sinister plan. I could not wait to exit the courtroom stage. My mind was racing while walking to take my seat in the jury box. Did Alex Murdaugh just give me a disarming smile attempting to curry favor? Did he think that I would be taken in by his seemingly gracious persona? Whatever it was, it only knocked me off my game for a moment because now all I could think was "Buddy, that is not how this is going to work. I will judge based on the evidence."

Alex was clearly absent from his law classes when they learned about *habeas corpus*, but he was confident in his understanding of *voir dire*. If you just said, "What in the world is she talking about?" Stop reading, grab some popcorn, and listen to *Murdaugh Murders Podcast*'s episode entitled "Incoming Call from Alex Murdaugh: The Jailhouse Tapes" (S01E33). You can thank me later. He knew exactly what he wanted in a jury but was sorely mistaken in thinking my verdict was susceptible to his manipulations.

Once all eighteen of us were in place, the clerk of court briefed us on basic day-to-day operations for the remainder of the trial. She told us where law enforcement would pick us up each morning so we could be transported to the courthouse together. She let us know snacks and drinks were always available, and lunch would be brought in each day. These protocols would be effective immediately. The juror's oath was administered, and we were dismissed for lunch. The Clerk of Court instructed us to take our cars to the secured area, and we would be transported back for opening statements.

It was very clear to us all that maintaining our safety and preserving the integrity of the case was paramount to the court. A few weeks prior to the trial's start date, Judge Newman issued an order seeking to protect jurors' anonymity, "by prohibiting the disclosure of their identity, along with certain relevant information pertaining to the jurors summoned to appear, and later serve, considering the nature of the case and in the interest of justice." Much to my relief, we were not sequestered in the traditional sense of being kept together and away from home. However, a partial sequestration was implemented, as an additional protective guardrail. This would allow us to sleep in our own bed at night, but we would remain a group travelling to and from the courthouse together during the weekdays. Each morning, we would park in a designated location and get shuttled to the courthouse. Because there were eighteen of us, we divided evenly between two blackout vans. We were transported to the courthouse by both an officer from the Colleton County Sheriff's Department and a bailiff. The vans would park around back where the staff and judge usually entered. Once we arrived, the vans backed into a tented area to keep us shielded from spectators and the media until it was time to go into the jury room.

For the ensuing six weeks, I would no longer be spending my weekdays as a payroll specialist; I would be making $20.00 per day fulfilling my civic duty at the Colleton County Courthouse. That meager amount would barely move the needle on the gas tank of my mid-size SUV, which made me even more grateful for the support of my colleagues and the paid time off they provided. I felt guilty knowing I would be leaving my small team in the lurch for *at least* three weeks, which ended up being twice that. So, when I returned home from the courthouse in the early evening, I would log on to our system and do anything I could to help them, especially during payroll weeks, as that was my primary role.

Helping my co-workers from afar when I was able was all I could do because now I was 1/12 of a team chosen to speak truth to power and be a voice for Maggie and Paul, as Lois Bujold reminds us, "The dead cannot cry out for justice. It is a duty of the living to do so for them."

CHAPTER 3:
LAWYERS, GUNS, AND MONEY

I don't think anyone would be shocked to hear that my time in the jury box was far from boring. There were witnesses who kept us rapt, flinging bombshell-after-bombshell our way, while others seemed like actors in the Dick and Jim show or extras in the prosecutions "trial within a trial." For example, the two-shooters of limited height tag team Mike Sutton and Tim Palmbach, made bank for co-starring in the defense's limited run of *One Killer, Two Guns—No Way*. Likewise, it did not take the testimony of about a dozen witnesses to convince us that when it came to stealing money, Alex had a strict non-discrimination policy. Three would have expressly convinced us Murdaugh *loved* himself first, money second, and the idea of loving close friends and family third. Determining a witness's believability was the cornerstone of our jury charge which read, "It is your duty to carefully examine and weigh the testimony of the witnesses and the evidence as a whole. You are the sole judge of the credibility of a witness and the weight to be given to their testimony... We the jury, reached our unanimous verdict of guilty by following all instructions provided by Judge Newman, prior to opening statements, during the trial, and after closing arguments.

It is truly a blessing to live in a country where *all* citizens have "rights guaranteed," ensuring even the most nefarious among us receives a fair trial. By design, The Fifth Amendment of the United States Constitution, shrouds the accused in a presumption of innocence. While the Sixth guarantees, "the rights of criminal defendants, including the right to a public trial without unnecessary delay; the right to a lawyer; the right to an impartial jury; and the right to know the accusers and nature of the charges and evidence against him." This is the gold standard Harpootlian clings to when questioned about choosing to represent Alex Murdaugh, as he reminds us, "John Adams, made the deeply unpopular decision to defend British troops on murder charges after the Boston Massacre. Abraham Lincoln defended nearly two dozen accused murderers as an Illinois lawyer before becoming president." Our system continues to thrive centuries later because of our forefathers' wisdom and the defense teams who vehemently uphold these securities.

As a quick reminder, I am a payroll specialist. The following analysis is based solely on my experience as a Murdaugh juror who operated under her solemn oath to follow the *evidence*. My objective is to explain the various elements which helped *me* arrive at a guilty verdict. Countless times it was said this was a complex and layered case. I could not agree more with the attorneys who stated—and restated—this during trial and the innumerable analysts who echoed their notion. My intention is *not* to offer a patronizing, agenda-driven rebuke of Team Murdaugh, but simply to put forward a lay discussion of their strategy and the impact it had on my understanding of the case.

Before arriving for the first day of jury selection, I had never heard of Jim Griffin and barely remembered Dick Harpootlian was a state senator. To help me better understand the tactics they used at trial, I decided to begin by exploring the evolution of their legal careers. Collectively, they had decades of knowledge that spanned both sides of the courtroom and had a familiarity with the unique curiosities of a high-profile case. Harpootlian has vast experience in cases involving violent crimes, while Griffin can boast the same for white collar offenses. With Alex facing sprawling indictments in both arenas, Dick and Jim seemed an ideal match. Prior to proceedings, *The Post and Courier* ran a series of articles that served to ready the public for the trial of the century. Avery Wilkes profiled the legal power couple, predicting what trial watchers might see from Harpootlian and Griffin:

Harpootlian will do opening statements, jump at every opportunity to tear into the state's theory of the case, and play a key role in cross-examining witnesses. As a trial lawyer, Harpootlian is known for laying traps for witnesses on the stand, by asking a series of questions which, on the surface, appear inane then catch the witness in a "gotcha" moment. Griffin, meanwhile, will use the rules of evidence to try and suppress what could be considered damaging. Griffin is known for digging through voluminous case files to find the slightest flaw in a criminal investigation that he can exploit at trial.

Dick and Jim followed this very playbook the reporters forecasted. I am not certain that even the newest, shiniest crystal ball could have predicted the detrimental blows the dream team would endure, not to mention countless fizzled gotchas, overruled objections, and failed attempts at discrediting and scapegoating multiple branches of law enforcement.

This odd couple brought a certain *je ne sais quoi* to the courtroom which Wilkes attributed to their differing approaches to litigation, "Harpootlian is a showman, and Griffin a no-nonsense grinder. Harpootlian loves media attention; Griffin looks squeamish in front of cameras. Harpootlian does not use notes but prefers to adapt as he reads the room, while Griffin is known to create slideshows and walk juries through complex issues." Impressive victories, varied experiences, as well as individualized and honed strengths presented a winning profile heavily lauded throughout the media and among their peers.

In rewatching key testimony and *in camera* discussions, I saw glimpses of the revered top-notch attorneys I'd heard so much about. Each time they'd edge toward a shocking, game changing Perry Mason moment, distortions and partial truths would instead uncover a school of red herring in the spirit of *My Cousin Vinny*.

Mere feet from us, day-after-day, Dick and Jim sought to plant seeds of reasonable doubt. In the early weeks of trial, Griffin and Harpootlian seemed like the formidable opponents trumpeted by media. Clever cross-examinations would often give me pause to reconsider previous testimony. For example, when Harpootlian was scrutinizing crime scene preservation, or rather lack there-of, with various witnesses from law enforcement, I began to see what could be considered genuine areas of concern, otherwise discounted by the state. Obviously, I cannot speak about the impact this may or may not have had on my fellow jurors, in that moment, because we consistently obeyed Judge Newman's instructions. However, I can now say, during deliberations, no one expressed concern for a botched investigation.

In addition, I found Harpootlian's practice of reiterating claims at fever pitch brash and pointless. This is no magic formula for making an assertion relevant or true. He seemed fixated on discrediting career detectives for imagined blunders they claim were constructed to implicate Alex Murdaugh in the murders of Maggie and Paul. Each time Harpootlian defaulted to the "shoddy police work" tactic, his accusations fell flat.

Dick's combative nature and caustic tone, simply put, were offensive. During cross-examination, he tried to make himself appear more knowledgeable than the expert, so much so that

I was *almost* embarrassed for him. Harpootlian acted like the pompous jerk who believes himself to be the smartest guy in the room—the type *everyone* loves to avoid. I understand there is an occasion where this strategy may work, and work well, but without fail, Dick chose the wrong witness at the wrong time. Trial watchers won't forget his mantrums about SLED's failure to wear booties to help preserve the crime scene. His repeated mention of them made it a hot button issue, which peaked when the defense's forensics expert, Kenneth Zercie, took the stand. Upon reviewing bodycam footage from Moselle on June 7, 2021, Dick asked, "Did you notice any protective covering on their feet? What, if anything, under the procedures you understand is the purpose of those?" Zercie then stated, "None of the officers appear to be wearing booties or 'shoe cots' inside the feed room. Wearing these is a basic precaution and should be standard operating procedure. They prevent contamination of the crime scene, including errant shoe prints and materials from the bottom of the police officers' shoes." Zercie finally uttered the words they'd waited five long weeks to hear. The defense latched onto this investigative faux pas and held it firm, just like Bubba when he clenches down on a chicken. Team Murdaugh's own witness would vindicate Dick and the paper shoe coverings he so greatly reveres.

There is a deep irony to this manufactured "told you so" testimony. Due to the humidity, rain, and blood-soaked crime scene, paper booties would have not held up, creating more of a mess. In a post-verdict interview with law enforcement, Captain Jason Chapman discussed Team Murdaugh's constant criticism of the investigation. He recognized mistakes were made and acknowledged that professionals learn and evolve with every experience. Likewise, Chapman commented that it was time for everyone to know the truth. Defending the work of detectives and first responders, he called attention to a few "mistakes" homed in on by the defense. Stressing some of them, in reality, were not mistakes at all and begins with "bootiegate:"

> The feed room is where they said we should have, by protocol, worn booties. There's only one way in the feed room and one way out, and all those contaminants are all over the front of that feed room. What is less likely to introduce contaminants into this crime scene, a rubber soled shoe or a paper bootie? A paper bootie is going to do nothing but soak up all that water, blood, and everything else. The first step taken in that room is going to transfer all that stuff from the paper bootie. Any crime scene class and any crime scene manual in the nation says to use only what is necessary. It is not common protocol to wear booties at a crime scene, especially one outdoors. I even asked other crime scene investigators in other jurisdictions when's the last time you wore booties in an exterior crime scene. You don't—because it's not the right tool for the job.

Oh, how I wish Captain Chapman would have had the opportunity to say this from the witness stand. Out of pure anger, Dick would have turned fifty shades of red, and I would have had a front-row seat. Then with wild abandon Harpootlian veered from the (somewhat) salient to the absurd, flinging allegations of crime scene impropriety at anyone who was in the vicinity of Moselle on the night of the murders. For a moment, I wondered if he might hurl such accusations at Bambi, Thumper, or Mr. Owl if they even crept near the kennels that evening.

Forensics expert, Special Agent Harpootlian, also showed the world his expertise in evidence collection, and his specialization in cellular technology. With bluster, Dick asked Agent Dalila Cirencione, then a crime investigator with SLED, "Have you ever heard of a Faraday bag?" . . . "Were you given any special instructions about handling the iPhone, other than putting it in a brown paper bag, 'like a can of pork and beans?'" When he went low, she went high, and politely replied, "No, but it would depend on if the pork and beans was considered evidence."[4] On direct examination, Lt. Britt Dove with SLED's computer crimes center, was asked about the bag. In one concise statement, he undercut its relevance and perceived importance to the case, affirming, "SLED's policy after collecting a cell phone is to place it in Airplane Mode and remove its SIM card—not inside a Faraday bag."

Amid their chaotic strategy of "attack the investigation," both Dick and Jim dabbled in misogyny, as they worked fiercely to humiliate and discredit two more female investigators. The indisputable expertise of Colleton County's Laura Rutland and SLED's Melinda Worley was an obvious threat to the defense. Rutland and Worley, among the entirety of law enforcement, provided early, powerful testimony which helped us complete the border of this challenging jigsaw puzzle. I don't mean to imply

Dick and Jim acted in a respectful manner to their male counterparts because that is simply untrue. Their behavior was equally as reprehensible, but was unique to many of the female witnesses, especially those who brought forward evidence they did not want us to hear. Dick and Jim's arrogance and aggression on cross-examination was excruciating to watch. When a female hijacked a potential Perry Mason moment, the defense refused to surrender. When Dick or Jim perceived *any* witness testimony as hazardous to their case, they'd flush, begin stammering and/or start talking in circles. If the threat happened to be a woman, without hesitation, they uncorked the misogyny which was otherwise suppressed, and started spewing sexist jabs.

Detective Laura Rutland and Special Agent Melinda Worley both provided evidence that vigorously contradicted the facts of their *first* theory. Due to its complexity and the passage of time, it is summarized below:

> From the moment the Colleton County Sheriff's office and SLED arrived at Moselle, they systematically worked together to keep Murdaugh in the investigative circle. Law enforcement aggressively questioned him, and he was a victim of their rush to judgement. They never considered any other suspects. Law enforcements' incompetence compromised the integrity of the crime scene which made it a hotbed of contamination.

The defense had woven an elaborate tale straight out of daytime television. It had blame deflection, conspiracy, and incompetence; it was only missing an evil twin, unrequited love, and quicksand. The dismantling of this outrageous theory began with Rutland's description of how Alex appeared unusually clean when she arrived on scene, just a couple of hours after he phoned emergency services. This observation contradicted Alex's insistence that he tried to roll Paul over to check for a pulse. Likewise, she detailed how the pools of blood surrounding him were undisturbed by foot or knee prints. As no surprise to trial watchers, Rutland showed herself to be exceedingly competent, which seemed to shock Jim Griffin. Once Rutland's replies could no longer erroneously be spun in favor of Alex, Griffin seemed to recoil in panic. Not ready to end the cross-examination, he moved to a personal attack. Previously on direct, John Meadors began by asking her to, "please tell the ladies and gentlemen of this jury about Laura Rutland. Where you're from; where you were born; where you lived, and a little bit of your background leading up to law enforcement." At one point during her introduction, she mentioned having a long-time interest in true crime. Jim must have deemed this taboo because he would move to discredit Rutland by misrepresenting her own words. His voice dripping with condescension and mired in sexism, Griffin tried to cheapen her career by implying she chose law enforcement because she was a "*CSI* junkie."

Confusing a Hollywood police procedural with the genre of true crime may seem like a minor misstatement to some, but such a conflation creates layers of bias. By doing this, he insulted her intelligence, questioned her competence, and implied she is unable to distinguish fact from fiction. True crime docuseries such as *Dateline*, *48 Hours*, and *20/20* are very different from sensationalized "ripped from the headlines" shows like *CSI*, *Law and Order*, and *NCIS*. True crime is grounded in the facts of the case and works tirelessly to keep victims and their stories in the forefront. I am very confident that neither Dick nor Jim would have the audacity to ask Dr. K (Kenny Kinsey) if he chose the field of forensics because he never missed an episode of *Bones*.

Likewise, Harpootlian's brazen resentment of facts was undeniable during his lengthy badgering, I mean cross-examination, of then Special Agent Melinda Worley. Most of Savanna Goude's questioning of the former Senior Criminologist from SLED, was dedicated to the introduction of evidence, which included, "additional photos, items collected at autopsy, and ammunition both fired and unfired found around the property. Worley also testified to taking swabs from various places on the driver's side of Murdaugh's black Suburban, which tested presumptive for blood, prompting agents to later collect the entire seatbelt."

As a woman and decent human, watching Harpootlian question Melinda Worley was painful. Dick, like Jim, reveled in any opportunity to take a bigoted swing at Worley's occupation asking, "What's so special about a special agent?" The gallery, not the jury box, erupted in laughter. Jodie Foster's doppelgänger, however, managed a quick smile, as she matter-of-factly replied, "It's just what SLED agents are called."

In the first few days of testimony, I questioned my own understanding of a defense attorney's role. It certainly could not be a profession that measured its most successful by how much hatred and rancor they could muster in the courtroom. I was relieved to learn reporter Michael Dewitt was also a bit troubled by Harpootlian's demeanor calling it an "often grueling cross-examination in which he grilled Worley with inquiries that questioned both state and local police practices, as well as the integrity of the crime scene and the evidence collected, including that of the footprints and ballistics taken at the scene"[9]

Dick used her testimony about bullet trajectory as a conduit for introducing another possibility into their kitchen sink defense. On the menu for day six, Dick teased "two shooters" as their theory *du jour*. Just like Laura Rutland, she pushed back, and when Dick asked, "Doesn't this indicate to you that there were two shooters? Is it possible that there were two shooters?" This was certainly not the "aha" or "gotcha" moment Harpootlian was accustomed to. With flat affect, and no further elaboration, she replied, "It just indicated there was movement." Special Agent Worley kicked off week two of testimony by dropping the mic, right on Dick's baby toe.

The defense's failed attempts at sullying Rutland and Worley's expertise only supersized their indignance. In no time, we had ringside seats to a battle royale of male egos. For a while there, it seemed Dick and Jim were competing with one another to see how fast and how far they could push a witness during cross-examination. Harpootlian leveled-up when he attempted to shred the credibility of Dr. Ellen Riemer, the pathologist who performed Maggie and Paul's autopsies. Whether Harpootlian was tossing hypotheticals at her, yammering about a muddy footprint on Maggie's calf, or bellowing about Paul having a contact wound, she remained stoic, which only fueled his outrage. Dick's behavior reminded me of my son at five-years-old, asking for ice cream over-and-over until he got it. However, there is one significant difference, he stopped after the third time I said no. Did he *really* think angering Dr. Riemer would undermine her brilliant testimony and debunk her credibility?

Dick and Jim might consider hostility an essential quality for any defense attorney, but I found it alienating. Once I was finally able to retire my alter ego, Juror 864, I found out many of my fellow jurors felt the same way. Likewise, their no holds barred commitment to discrediting witnesses only made them look weak, time and again. I don't disagree, this approach can be effective, but only in the case of an *appropriate* witness, like Alex Murdaugh who suffers from debilitating "lieabetes." Ambushing someone with more credentials than Dick has petty jabs for Eric Bland is never a good idea.

Team Murdaugh's Phil Barber, the bearded fellow who is seen but seldom heard, must have lost a game of *Roshambo* during the defense's morning huddle, as he was tasked with challenging DNA expert Sara Zapata and Lt. Britt Dove, SLED's computer crimes analyst. Paper obviously covered rock the two times Dr. K. took the stand, as Dick and Jim were each given the chance to undermine the testimony of a man whose resume is longer than a CVS receipt. So much so, when Dick's petulant inner child grew tired of listening to his credentials, devoid of restraint, he interrupted proceedings to quip, "I'll concede to him being qualified as an expert witness if Waters will just get this over with."

Secondly, the meandering threads of Dick and Jim's web of alternative theories, often felt like a *Choose Your Own Adventure* book. It did not take them long to realize the homicide/suicide theory was ridiculous. That gamble ended almost as quickly as it began. Charlie Condon concedes, "Their seemingly chaotic approach may have been the result of leaning too heavily on the outcomes from pre-trial focus groups. These tests consistently showed difficulty in believing the prosecution's claim he murdered Maggie and Paul to distract from his financial crimes." Long after Condon made that statement, Jim Griffin and his tarnished ego, repeated a similar sentiment on the CW's *Crime Nation* saying, "We thought the state did not have enough forensic evidence to prove guilt. Secondly, why would one person bring two guns to a murder? That does not make any sense." Dick and Jim worked tirelessly to poke holes in the state's narrative, but they seemed to drown in their own abyss of hogwash. The pair continually failed to show reasonable doubt, largely because every hypothetical they proposed, there was never a logical throughline. However, day-after-day, the one thing we could count on hearing was "Alex was a good father and loving husband." Alas, for Dick and Jim, the refrain never caught on and just lay bare their desperation. How could we, the jury, believe in Alex's innocence when his own defense team seemed incapable of convincing themselves.

Over the six weeks, I could never figure out if they were operating from a blueprint or improvising, and it was never more evident than when they used the kitchen sink strategy of tossing everything in, hoping something would stick. This is not unlike another of their preferred tactics which pop-culture patois refers to as the "Chewbacca Defense." A brief remediation on *Star Wars* reminds us Chewbacca was Han Solo's adorably tall, hairy sidekick who could only speak in his native language. However, he understands English making Han the perfect companion because he knows Chewie's language perfectly. As this relates to trial, *Wikipedia* explains it as "a propaganda strategy devised to overwhelm and confuse listeners with senseless arguments to drown out the sensible ones." Team Murdaugh tried this frequently, and we will never know if it was of an intricate defense strategy, or if they just thought we were eighteen easily confused dirt road morons.

If either of those became too tedious, Dick and Jim sped straight on to cruelty. Many trial watchers, I'm sure, cringed as soon as Harpootlian stood to begin his cross-examination of Tony Satterfield. He is the eldest son of Gloria, the Murdaugh's deceased housekeeper who helped raise Buster and Paul, allowing Alex and Maggie to enjoy their jet-set lifestyle. As Dick approached the podium, all I could think was, "Oh, no, this is going to be bad." I said a prayer for Tony. It was just as vile as I imagined, but he held his own. Tony may appear small in stature but has a devout abiding faith and an independent spirit which sets him towering above others. So much so, that he would not allow Dick Harpootlian's animus to intimidate or break him. Gigi McKelvey, host of the podcast *Pretty Lies and Alibis*, described this uncomfortable encounter for her listeners, "Dick asked him something, cuts him off and interrupts, 'oh I'm sorry, you're not a lawyer.' I thought it was very demeaning; he talked down to him and people behind me made audible noises." She continued by offering her listeners a glimpse into our hearts and minds during Tony's distressing testimony:

Harpootlian did not win any points with the jury. They did not appreciate this line of questioning. When asked why he agreed to let Alex help him, Tony said, 'I trusted him.' I'm going to tell you every eye on that jury went right to Alec. They stared him down. They took well to Tony, and when he left, every member of that jury watched him walk out, and several of them had a very faint smile on their face, like good for you dude.

I can say Gigi perfectly described the vibe that pulsated throughout the entire jury box.

Months later Tony gave a victim's impact statement at Alex's sentencing for the financial crimes, and told him, "You lied, cheated and stole, but I forgive you and will pray for you." Gloria would be so proud of the outstanding young man he has become.

I don't think there is a better way to conclude this chapter than with this sentiment from Reddit user "Betty Bowers," who, nearly two years prior to trial, forecast a disastrous dénouement for Murdaugh's dream team when she posted, "Perhaps, Harpootlian, who is so used to smugly, smoothly spinning all types of implausible tales to gullible audiences, has gotten himself a client so evil this time that even Dick and Jim won't be able to palm off, on reasonable people, the imaginative fiction of far-fetched innocence." Her prescient words have proven timeless. Richard Alexander Murdaugh remains the kryptonite for the dynamic duo, and any courtroom where they are his acting defense counsel becomes their Alamo.

CHAPTER 4:
TIL' THE LAW SAYS STOP

When this double-murder case landed in Attorney General Alan Wilson's office, he immediately recognized the massive undertaking; while remaining vigilantly aware its outcome was equally as proportionate, if not greater. A just verdict could end the cycle of corruption which loomed over the South Carolina Lowcountry for over eight decades, forever altering the legal landscape of our state's Fourteenth Judicial Circuit. Knowing the gravity, AG Wilson's first step was to appoint the indefatigable Creighton Waters as lead prosecutor. From there, a bevy of men and one *woman*, without fear or favor, would take their position on the front line as the designated pursuers of justice for Maggie and Paul. Their immense respect for one another, witnesses, the rule of law, and those who protect it, spawned a crew so exceptional, it seemed Lady Justice climbed from atop her pedestal and handpicked them. Although, we would end up hearing from some, more than others, no one was napping on the prosecution side, yet it appeared the same could not be said for opposing counsel. Due to the mammoth size of the team, I can't speak to each, but instead will focus on those who best brought the case to life—for me— leaving an indelible impression that would not soon fade and include Creighton Waters, John Meadors, and Savanna Goude.

From his first words during opening statements to his last at closing arguments, it was not difficult to see the passion Creighton Waters brought to the courtroom. He had an energy which continually sent shockwaves throughout the jury box. No matter the task, whether a meticulously developed direct examination, fiery cross, or prone on the floor demonstrating bullet trajectory, he vigorously delivered every single day. Commenting further on this powerhouse, reporter Avery Wilks says, "he has built a reputation as a tireless investigator, a tenacious negotiator and a legal wizard committed to delivering justice to the bad guys." Creighton Waters was the perfect choice to spearhead this team, as he is the embodiment of all that is conspicuously absent in Murdaugh World. *The Post and Courier* did a profile on the lead prosecutor, where friends and colleagues commented on the staunch moral code he has held from a very young age. The story I feel that most characterizes the Creighton Waters we spent six weeks with at the Colleton County Courthouse is one recounted by his childhood friend, Zeke Bennet. He tells of the time Creighton's head collided with his face while playing football on an undeveloped lot. This crash resulted in a bloody nose, which Zeke revealed, Waters is still apologizing for decades later, as "Doing what he perceives to be the wrong thing really bothers him." From a makeshift football field to the courtroom well, Creighton is steered by his trusty moral compass. We witnessed this unwavering integrity, time and again, both at trial and throughout the myriad of Murdaugh's hearings which followed our guilty verdict.

Just as the world watched Waters doggedly pursue the Lowcountry's most famous miscreant, it is important to know his commitment to justice pertains to any, and all, offenders. Columbia defense attorney, Greg Harris, shares the following anecdote about an awkward plea deal he tried to broker with Creighton:

> Harris asked Waters to consider a light sentence for his client, a former state Department of Transportation employee. Waters had indicted him in a corruption sting that had made statewide headlines. He balked at Harris's proposition brusquely telling him, 'I can't do that because that result is not going to stop the next guy from doing this very same thing.'

Imagine, just for a moment, that attorney Harris wanted to negotiate the same deal, *but* with Alex Murdaugh playing the starring role of prosecutor. The lighter sentence would have swiftly been granted, but at a price that would result in *both* Harris and his client owing Alex. And likely not while the ink is still wet, for every deal with Murdaugh is on his terms and has no expiration date. The world needs more emissaries of light like Creighton Waters and far fewer harbingers of darkness like Alex, who has left an indelible smear on the profession—one so severe Judge Newman mentioned it *both* times Alex stood before him, as did Judge Gergel when he oversaw his federal sentencing, saying before a packed courtroom, "a law license is a license to do good, what you've done demonstrates the darker side of holding a license to practice law." With the same logic Waters offered Harris, Gergel submitted to Alex, asserting "The purpose of this lengthy sentence, is to deter others from committing similar conduct." However, the stain will only continue to set and eventually become permanent unless McCormick's most famous inmate, his merry band of thieves, and his unscrupulous enablers stop creating breaking news.

Most of my six weeks of service centered on testimony about the brutal murders of Maggie and Paul. We listened thoroughly as the prosecution led us down the serpentine path which ended at the kennels on that hot and humid Lowcountry night. However, consistently running in the background of Murdaugh's labyrinth of lies were his financial crimes.

As the principal prosecutor, Waters seemed to bear the brunt of media criticism for the number of witnesses called and how much trial time their testimony consumed. So much so, an independent media outlet branded it "the trial within a trial." Feedback, at large, equated to, and I summarize, "Enough already; we get it. This is a murder trial!" I don't disagree entirely and feel for the trial watchers who sat through that testimony twice. I am, however, grateful for the cross section of witnesses which included his victims, like Tony Satterfield; law firm staff (Jeanne Seckinger and Annette

Griswold); law partners (Ronnie Crosby and Mark Ball); corporate bigwigs, such as Jan Malinowski (EVP of Palmetto State Bank) and Michael Gunn (Principal at Forge Consulting) to lifelong friends like Chris Wilson. I understood Waters's goal was to prove motive, as well as help us fully grasp the breadth of his deception and the depth of Alex's avarice. It would take several people to illustrate the complexities of his schemes and just how far the tentacles spread. Through these witnesses collectively, we could see a man devoid of all compunction with an absolute disregard for others—emotionally and financially. Realizing the magnitude of this scheming, and his scorched earth approach, the defendant's motive became crystal clear to me and my fellow jurors. As the prosecution said, or at least implied, almost daily, "If he'd lie to them, he'd lie to us." Alex Murdaugh was trapped in a Ground Hog Day of deceit which seemingly should have ended after three sentencing hearings. However, results of the latest mandatory polygraph, administered almost thirteen months, to the day, from our guilty verdict, indicated that Pinocchio's prison-issued orange pants are still ablaze.

Creighton Waters delivered an intense, powerful closing argument, which supplied us with an outline of the elements we needed to consider during deliberation. He focused on the three "indicators of suspicion" used by law enforcement to determine the course of an investigation—motive, means, and opportunity. To this triad, Waters would also add guilt of conscience. He also reminded us of the case's complexity, which had almost as many layers as a Russian Nesting Doll. Yet, it was the weight Alex placed on legacy that would turn his family history into a Southern Gothic reprisal of Truman Capote's *In Cold Blood*.

Seasoned veteran, John Meadors brought an unforgettable energy every time he stood to take the podium, no matter if he was on direct or cross examination. Meadors joined the team just a few weeks before the trial began, bringing with him 35 years' worth of experience in exclusively trying murder cases. His passion for the law, and by that, I mean—law, like follow the rules kind of law—*not* defend a client by badgering witnesses, misstating facts, and acting foolish. Additionally, the unrehearsed and genuine empathy he felt for their witnesses during trial was palpable. One example that immediately comes to mind is Shelley Smith. When she became emotional on the stand, he paused, warmly asking, "Why are you crying, Ms. Smith?" These six little words had to mean so much to her during that difficult testimony she was obviously bereft and reluctant to provide. This gave her a chance to show the world how much she cared for the family and how it was tearing her apart to be disloyal, which only increased her believability. The prosecution team joked that "Alex was the worst witness against Alex." I agree with this statement 100%. Nevertheless, if that were not the case, and I was forced to reveal the exact moment I knew Alex was lying—it would have been when he claimed, "Ms. Shelley must have been mistaken about how long I was there." To which I wanted to stand up and shout, "No! No, Sir. I know you did not try to call that godly woman a liar."

Of *SC vs. Alex Murdaugh*, John Meadors said, "My focus was on the witnesses and the emotion of it; that's what I love doing." He personified this sentiment with Ms. Shelley, giving millions of trial watchers a glimpse into John Meadors—the person—showing them the ardent sensitivity which informs his livelihood. I don't mean to imply that Creighton Waters and Savanna Goude, and every other member of the superb team, lacked sincerity, as that would be categorically false. It is just that their defined areas of focus did not offer as much opportunity to lay bare such sentiment. Secondly, when Mr. Meadors's turn for questioning either followed, or preceded, a particularly vicious assault by the defense, he shined that much brighter.

I'd be telling a story, if I neglected to say that some of us were sometimes jarred by his constant movement and up-close approach when questioning witnesses. Mr. Meadors certainly kept us alert, almost like we were watching a tennis match. Moving our heads side-to-side as he walked up and down the length of the jury box. Another thing that often came as a surprise was Dick's propensity to wander the well, inserting himself into the prosecution's demonstratives at the most unexpected times. Dick Harpootlian is an enigma, acting, at times, like the legendary attorney who prosecuted South Carolina's most famous mass murderer Pee Wee Gaskins, while at others, as Michael Dewitt observed, "he looked like a man who had lost his car keys, fumbling for exhibits and delaying the courtroom action."

I found it quite humorous that the trait we most noticed in Mr. Meadors was raised by Anne Emerson of WCIV, she inquired, "I want to discuss your style of working with the witnesses on the stand and the jury, as well. It was different from what we've seen from other attorneys—much closer and the cameras couldn't follow you. Does it literally help to get just right there with them it was such a unique way of speaking?"

Not at all slighted or taken aback by her query, in his southern drawl, he graciously replied:

> I'd like to move right now, to be honest with you, but I know we can't. It's nothing planned. I've told some lawyers over my life, 'you just got to be yourself.' I'm literally reacting in the moment. I don't think about it, and I apologize if I move too much. My dad, who's a retired Methodist Bishop, and the best speaker I've ever seen—he's fantastic. Early in my career, I'd move. Some people said, 'you can't do that.' He finally said, 'just be yourself, son.' So I do just that, and I feel better when I move about, and am just reacting in the moment and listening to the witnesses, which is so important as a lawyer.

Hearing the story behind his perpetually *moving* courtroom demeanor was endearing. It is not hard to recognize the influence his father had on his success as a skilled orator. He would elaborate further on this in his closing and include his mother. Speaking about the positive influences of language and reading he told us, "My father gave me the book *Your Greatest Power* by J. Martin Kohe. In this the author claims, 'A person's greatest power is the power to choose.' Similarly, he shares of when his mother sent him off to college with a copy of *The Velveteen Rabbit*, where inside, she inscribed the simple lesson, 'Always be real.'" Through recounting the lessons learned from these treasured gifts, he brought it full circle back to Alex, then concluded with an empowering plea directed to the twelve of us. He summed up the case's foundation as one of "common sense" which all comes down to "credibility and believability" encouraging us to use our "everyday life experiences to weigh the evidence and ultimately determine who is telling the truth."

Lastly, Meadors suggested since there is no manual to being a juror, that we use the two books he mentioned as our guide. Offering a spoiler, he stated, Kohe claims, "our greatest power, is the power to choose." Then Mr. Meadors continued, "we make decisions, both good and bad, every day of our lives and must live with the consequences of those decisions. But Alex loved himself and the lavish lifestyle he built on lies and fraud more than his wife and son. He exercised his greatest power of choice to make sure that life continued, or at least tried to." While *The Velveteen Rabbit* is about what it means to be real, and Richard Alexander Murdaugh was "a defendant who was never real; his defense attorneys blamed everybody else but the man who lied to investigators and his family, as he desperately to conceal the truth — he killed Maggie and Paul." Alex looked countless people in the eye while blatantly lying; John Meadors, however, left us with these final words, "Now it's time for you—the jury—to exercise your greatest power—the power to reach a verdict to find Murdaugh guilty and end his lies once and for all." At the end of the impassioned monologue, that man deserved a standing ovation. I had to resist the urge to toss imaginary roses at him while shouting "Bravo," as he stood slightly breathless on the courtroom floor. When curious trial watchers would ask my thoughts about his closing, I would *jokingly* reply, "The juror in seat #11 is no fun. She would not join me in a round of applause and shout encore."

Since it was the state's case to lose, for the burden of proof rests solely on them, they were granted this opportunity to present a concluding argument, or a rebuttal, to the points made by the defense. I had the opportunity to speak with Creighton Waters, and asked, "Why Mr. Meadors; did you just know he'd be the one to deliver the most powerful rebuttal?" In summation, he replied, it is always best to have multiple voices tell the story. The defense wanted that as well, but I argued against it because the rules don't allow it. However, the state is entitled to a concluding argument. Having known Meadors for years and worked with him before, he seemed like a good fit for the job. Everyone had their designated role, Savanna was on evidence, David, "my right-hand man," was primarily on ballistics, and John was the emotion man on the team. With his instinctual son of a preacher man cadence and innate fervor, he knocked it out of the park. After Creighton Waters masterfully condensed six weeks of testimony into *almost* 3 hours, he'd built us a lovely Neapolitan sundae, each flavor separate, yet relevant. While the only thing Jim Griffin appeared capable of creating was a viscous, dense mud pie—that did not impress a single one of us. Mr. Waters gave us the perfect parting gift by adding John Meadors to the trial's thunderous conclusion—he was the whipped cream and cherry topper for the sundae Creighton had scooped out earlier.

Like the flurry of locomotion that is signature to Meadors, so were the comments on YouTube. I am not sure what was more impressive, the closing itself or that in almost 1,400 comments, no user had anything cruel, irrelevant, or preposterous to say. Below is a smattering of the internet's praise, which I think captures the gamut of emotions we were feeling in those final hours:

Tigerlily9981: Historic closing. A prosecution team at its very finest. This entire case should be watched from beginning to end by every law student.

Munsy42: Mr. Meaders (sic) took us to church and brought a revival of Justice!!! I could listen to this man for hours!!! He is amazing!!

westernhemisphere2205: I've been watching cases for over 30 years, and this is literally one of the best closing arguments I've ever heard. This man is passionate and brilliant.

zoer7338: This guy is fantastic. He's speaking to all of the things that have been bugging me about the actions of Alex Murdaugh. It's just common sense observations. Common sense points the finger at the killer.

flightwife1828: The most moving, touching, amazing rebuttal closing argument I've ever heard. This is a man who knows exactly how to tell the story to reach & touch the jury. He did a wonderful job.

mariedibuono8932: Mr. Meadors deserves an Oscar for best argument by a prosecutor. He reminded me of Colombo.

stacieknock5828: This is Legal Opera; What a Lovely TAKE DOWN

barbaramartin5931: John Meadors gave me the Doors of the Church are now Open feeling by the time he closed I was wiping my eyes and knew he had put a lock on it. And the Jury didn't mess around with that verdict. Kudos to them.

Well, Mr. Meadors, I do believe you silenced the harshest critics, loudest trolls, and even the neediest provocateurs. It should not be discounted that for just over fifty-eight minutes the world and internet seemed to agree on two things—1) your rebuttal was Dy-No-Mite 2) that Alex Murdaugh dude is 100% guilty. However, amidst this epic dismantling, three outliers sat incensed in the courtroom that afternoon. With lips pursed and brows furrowed, Alex's soulless black eyes stared daggers at John Meadors, while Dick and Jim each appearing thoroughly gobsmacked, could only muster a vacuous scowl of defeat.

Savanna was the sole female dynamo for the prosecution. For someone who commanded the floor as she did, it is difficult to believe she was ever intimidated by the thought of law school. Growing up in a small South Carolina town, with very few lawyers, it seemed almost foreign to her. However, Savanna's interest was piqued after taking a constitutional law class. Considering our everyday lives are impacted by such regulations, Savanna decided to work in a law office one summer and then knew she had found her purpose and began her legal career at the now infamous 14th Circuit Solicitor's Office in 2016. Two short years later, she began working for the South Carolina Attorney General's Office in the State Grand Jury Division. There she would earn the respect of veteran attorneys and the nickname, "The Pit Bull." Creighton Waters, in an interview, acknowledges this was not the most flattering of monikers but the only way he could think to best describe her determined, strong-willed approach to work and the assertive way she takes hold of a difficult cross-examination. Of Savanna, Waters said, "This crime scene was difficult because a master manipulator was in charge of it. Savanna had an extremely tough job of doing and managing that. She's such a hard worker, and that was huge for me." This was an especially unique undertaking, as in this case the most relatable and damaging evidence was from digital forensics. However, Waters's unwavering belief in Goude was obvious in assigning her the very important role of authenticating the physical evidence, such as shell casings, shoes, and DNA swabs, for the record. Because the defense, in general, often bandies about allegations of evidence mishandling or hurls unabashed false claims that law enforcement manufactures evidence—like Dick and Jim so famously did—makes this a crucial role for both witness and attorney, as described below:

Identification of the Exhibit: Establishing the authenticity of real evidence. When a witness will testify to their familiarity with the object by recognition of it from a previous encounter and by the identification of it as the same from collection.

Establish Chain of Custody: This most often becomes a factor if evidence tampering is a concern (either real or imagined). The attorney, through testimony, will establish a proper chain of custody to show that the exhibit is identical and unaltered. In a criminal case this is done with testimony from police officers and/or crime scene technicians.

We saw this requisite and behemoth undertaking at play during the testimony of Melinda Worley from SLED. An independent media platform noted, Savanna Goude, "led her through the introduction of several dozen pieces of evidence." Regarding the significance of Agent Worley's testimony, and others of the like, someone with knowledge of the case stated to reporters, "There's a lot of mechanical witnesses—I wouldn't call them boring—but they are necessary."

Continuing by equating such evidence to a thousand-piece puzzle that does not make much sense at first, "but will make sense when they're tied together in a story."

Days after sentencing, WCIV had the opportunity to sit down with the prosecutorial team, in the very place the Grand Jury affirmed the four murder-related indictments of Alex Murdaugh. The room, painted in dark hues, showed five chairs in a line with both the American and South Carolina state flag serving as the backdrop. As the program opened, Savanna is seen in a skirt and blazer with numerous sports and suitcoats to her left. This is not unlike the Supreme Court portrait where Ruth Bader Ginsburg, donning her dissent collar, stands among her fellow colleagues—who are all male and number eight. Though this image of Savanna is on a smaller scale, minus judicial garb, it is no less consequential. For Goude could savvily—although the defense might think I meant savagely—bring objectivity to the grossly objectionable when on cross. For example, she was unafraid and unapologetic when it came to challenging bogus testimony, exposing its costly price tag, and revealing to us just exactly how they misrepresented the *facts*. She smoothly began cross on Timothy Palmbach by verifying his credentials. Savanna did so in a respectful and formal address, while feigning a lilt of uncertainty, as she quizzically asked, "Dr. Palmbach?" The witness had no choice but to respond. Falling all over his words, he sputtered, "No, I'm not a doctor!" Unflinching, she kept composed, tossed in a sprinkle of southern charm (for good measure) and genially said, "I just want to get it right." Mr. Palmbach was unaware that Savanna's intent was to just quickly remind us of his credentials; after which, she magnificently called into question several of his claims, upending each one. He remained oblivious that with every passing inquiry, she was systematically shredding his resume into a million little pieces, then tossing it up into the air like confetti, as he exited the witness stand.

When asked about why she was drawn to this case, Goude succinctly replied, "Just the defendant himself—someone in a trusted position, someone with power, and even a father. How could you do something like this? Going after people like him is why we do what we do."

In an "X" from Michael Dewitt, he commented, "brave women helped bring down Alex Murdaugh." This is an astute observation, as it was exceedingly true for many female witnesses, as well as Savanna herself.

There is an innate hardship that comes with being the only woman in a largely male environment. When face-to-face with such a gender imbalance in the workplace, most women reflexively feel they must work harder to be heard and taken seriously, or otherwise risk being looked at as just another pretty woman. Whether the disparity—real or imagined—happens in the local trade school's Tires and Breaks 110 class, on a sport's team, or behind the doors of justice, a female will likely feel subpar because the "boys club" still thrives—especially in the south. Women must always be on guard, cautious not to traverse the imaginary line of demarcation separating the well-respected, stalwart female attorney from an overly ambitious, bossy, nasty woman who happened to pass the bar exam. I can imagine this was compounded for Savanna who was forced to tread this invisible, fickle line on a remarkably large and public stage during the Lowcoutry's trial of the century. Until someone can locate, isolate, and delineate its exact positioning, women will continue to feel slighted, regardless of being the best person to ask questions of, if not solve a problem entirely.

When Savanna Goude talked, the world listened. She was undaunted by the voluminous physical evidence that had to be trudged through with many witnesses. Nor was she intimidated by dense and technical testimony, like the DNA evidence, which could have inspired, even the most zealous trial watcher, to take a lunch break or maybe even a power nap. It is not my intention to knock DNA experts, Lady Justice and jurors need them, but my unsolicited advice is this—bright-colored charts, focused on

THE LONG ROAD TO JUSTICE

only relevant numbers and/or contributors, and maybe a relatable analogy or two. Brilliant scientists, if you are reading this, we appreciate you, but most of us don't understand the majority of what you're saying. Moreover, the only existent fact we know about the difference between an octillion and a bajillion, is the latter is not a number.

Her response to my question, "Who was the most memorable witness" momentarily took me aback, but not in a bad way. However, what she said made a lot of sense. Savanna explained, "For me, Buster's testimony and presence at trial stands out. He must know what his father did and made the choice to support him. That speaks volumes in how far this family will go to try to protect their reputation." Her insight was eye-opening to me and provided a direct throughline to the prosecution's assertion that the legal scion "is the kind of person for whom shame is an extraordinary provocation' and when faced with financial ruin his ego couldn't stand it."

Upholding the family name at any cost was the principle which sustained the Murdaugh family for generations and still proved to be alive and thriving during Buster's time on the witness stand. In addition to protecting his father, he also made one final attempt to do what Alex did not get a chance to do—clear Paul's name. Jim asked Buster, "Did the family support Paul in the criminal matter." To which Buster answered, "Yes sir; we supported him in his criminal case because among the family, none of us thought that he was driving the boat when the accident occurred." Dr. John Matthias, forensic psychologist, and co-host of the podcast *Hidden True Crime*, uses Buster's testimony as a platform to illustrate enmeshment, a dysfunctional family dynamic. Where its members are over concerned and over involved in each other's lives. In extreme cases, the separation from the family is considered an act of betrayal. Belonging to the unit prevails over all other experiences and at the expense of each member's self-development. In enmeshed families there's a tremendous premium placed on loyalty because they are so closely aligned with one another. Dr. John continues by drilling down further with his analysis:

> It was a fairly concise and quick moment in Buster's testimony that gives tremendous insight into both the trial of Alex and the family. In addition to the Beach's lawyer, Mark Tinsley, hiring a bio mechanical engineer who proved there was no physical way Paul was *not* at the helm that night, every other living witness in the boat (Conner, Anthony, Morgan, and Miley) pointed the finger at Paul as the driver. Buster's testimony reveals—no matter what the facts are; no matter what the evidence is, they're going to deny those and stick together to perpetuate the family myth of power, perfection and being above the law, even if that success comes at the expense of incriminating Conner Cook—an innocent passenger whose life was changed forever because of Paul's recklessness.

Savanna's perception of Buster's testimony as a defense witness coupled with Dr. John's psychological explication offered profound insight into what motivated Alex daily, ultimately pushing him to do the unthinkable—slay his wife and youngest son.

Savanna Goude impressed trial watchers all over the globe with her pivotal role in the double murder trial. She was even memorialized on a series of coffee mugs that read Lowcountry Justice League and featured Judge Newman, sword in hand, lifting the scales of justice. On the days Savanna was up, she won the internet:

gscott00: There are big things in store for her. She did great to be so young on such a large stage.

MurdaughMerch: CONGRATULATIONS Savanna Goude! An excellent litigator, role model, and genuine bad mama jama. You went toe to toe with the most powerful men of their generation - and.you.won!

EgyptianMomma: Savanna Goude is hard core!! I really like her style

ArchetypeReader: Savanna Goude was great. I was impressed by her. She's so young but she held her own and was really good with witnesses. Well done!

DHVXIII: Very professional. She's gonna go far.

Creighton Waters, and his adept prosecutorial team, had one *consistent* narrative and shared the single goal of getting justice for Maggie and Paul. In addition to that, their healthy respect for law enforcement helped provide a solid foundation, which seemed to be missing from Murdaugh World. Emphasizing the financial crimes *and* letting Alex drive his own cross-examination, proved not to be prosecutorial missteps, but an intentional strategy that ultimately fulfilled their intent—showing motive—toppling Alex Murdaugh's criminal house of cards indefinitely.

CHAPTER 5:
CAN I GET A WITNESS?

"Circumstantial evidence is *still* evidence" was a phrase we, the jury, and millions of Murdaugh trial watchers heard *ad nauseum*. There were NO fingerprints, or DNA to implicate Alex in these atrocities and any gunshot residue could easily be explained away. Afterall, he obtained a gun for his protection soon after coming upon Maggie and Paul's lifeless bodies.

In a post-trial interview, the prosecution was asked which witnesses they felt were most impactful in propelling jurors to their guilty verdict. Creighton Waters noted the witnesses were either personal or expert, but both equally and effectively contributed to their narrative. Likewise, exhaustive research suggested a similar divide among legal analysts when asked about the evidence they found most compelling.

The prosecution was widely criticized for putting forth a motive many pundits felt absurd, unfathomable, and difficult to prove, especially with an absence of forensic evidence. It is largely thought the 24/7 saturation of police procedurals and true crime docuseries have led jurors astray with the heavy emphasis they place on the importance of forensics. Its impact is so pervasive it has created a phenomenon legal scholars have dubbed the *CSI* effect. In a nightly news interview, Creighton

Waters asserted, "Because people watch the show, they believe every case has some sort of magic type forensic evidence, but it doesn't always. During the opening, I pulled out my cell phone and said, 'There's a different type of forensic evidence, and that's the cell phone,' and this was crucial not just for the kennel video but the timeline as well." Research shows this can be a real problem in courtrooms, ending in a miscarriage of justice. Obviously, that was not the case for this jury. The prosecution's copious evidence *plus* our common sense *plus* our intellect would *equal* justice for Maggie and Paul. We, the jury, proved very capable of evaluating the credibility of witnesses and understanding the intricate testimony which described the digital footprints left by Paul, Maggie, and Alex on that dark, desolate country road connecting Moselle to Almeda.

I: EXPERT WITNESSES:

The state was not short on experts, and for that we were very grateful. Dr. Kenny Kinsey, Dr. Ellen Riemer and Special Agent Peter Rudofski were remarkable witnesses. From the testimony of Kenny Kinsey, it was easy to visualize the murders as if they were happening in real time, along with that of Dr. Riemer who recounted its brutality. While Special Agent Rudofski solidified and finalized a timeline for June 7, 2021, showing the entirety of Alex's physical movements from the time he left for work (around Noon) until he arrived back at Moselle and called 911 at 10:05 p.m.

Dr. Kenny Kinsey: High profile trials seem to have a unique way of producing their own celebrities. The double murder trial of Alex Murdaugh was no exception, and Kenny Kinsey, Orangeburg's self-proclaimed "Andy Griffith with a crime scene background" would have instantly earned his star on the trial watchers Walk of Fame, if there were such a thing. Genuine affability, with the soul of an educator made him the perfect expert witness. From the moment "Dr. K" took the stand, we knew his proficiency would clear up any confusion about what happened at Moselle on that balmy June night.

Watching cross-examinations of the prosecution's expert witnesses was often more difficult to sit through than it was informative. Watching it for the second time, to refresh my recollection for this chapter, was excruciating. I had forgotten how frequently I wanted to stand up and yell, "Objection; badgering the witness." Defense tactics are defense tactics—I know—but the browbeating many had to endure was horrible. The simple country lawyer schtick Dick pulled while questioning Dr. K. was mind-numbing. Initially, Harpootlian seemed prepared, and, dare I say, respectful. Then in an abrupt pivot, he segued into acting like a bullheaded class clown in a high school trigonometry class. Shout out to Dr. K.; if that teaching criminology thing gets boring, he'd make an excellent math instructor. With the patience of Job, he persevered, just to be called back days later as a rebuttal witness. Only this time, it would be Jim performing the role of backwoods southern lawyer. His inane questions at least provided trial watchers with the dark comic relief of a Southern Gothic novel:

Griffin: [*with swollen machismo*] How would a shot pellet get there?

Dr. K: [*stupefied and taken aback by the redundancy*] It's . . . Really??? I mean, ugh huh. The Cone. It's a cone, Mr. Griffin. I . . . I've already described how shot pattern works. It's a cone!

Griffin: [*puffed up like your Memaw's biscuits*] So it just missed his head, you think?

Dr. K: [*exasperated*] No, No. It come out of his head.

For six weeks, we watched the defense's buffoonery. If we were to add up the time Dick and Jim spent asking meaningless questions over-and-over again, the trial may have concluded in three weeks, as originally projected. I am certain most everyone who watched the trial shares my sentiment when I say, that is one dog and pony show we hope to never have the unfortunate experience of witnessing *ever again*.

Dr. Ellen Riemer: Without a doubt, the day Dr. Riemer, a forensic pathologist from the Medical University of South Carolina, testified was one of the hardest—for each one of us. With vivid details, she explained her findings at autopsy and did so in a manner which could be easily understood to people without a science background. Dr. Riemer was keenly aware that her primary audience of sixteen had a limited knowledge of anatomy which did not extend much beyond the obligatory frog dissection. None of us had abandoned a patient on the operating table to attend jury duty. She, like Dr. K, has immeasurable experience, profound knowledge, and the natural ability to make the complex understandable. This awareness is a commendable trait for any expert, as it is easy to get caught up in specialized language, often causing more confusion than understanding.

Since day one of testimony, through body camera footage and law enforcement's crime scene pictures, we had a distinct visual of the kennel's macabre tableau. It was week four when Dr. Riemer was sworn in, and we knew her testimony would not only be emotionally difficult, but also graphic. Fiona Guy, writer for the resource website *Crime Traveler*, notes this "evidence can be the most harrowing part of a murder trial." Having survived this phase of trial without being the retcher or retchee, there was nothing hyperbolic about her sentiment. Gigi McKelvey, host of the podcast *Pretty Lies and Alibis*, was doing double duty as a correspondent for *Law and Crime* during the Murdaugh trial. At the end of each day, she would provide listeners with a daily summation of testimony and include her courtroom observations. On the episode covering Dr. Riemer's testimony, she was extraordinarily empathetic to us. We were obviously at the front of her mind that day. Throughout the entire show, Gigi interjected sentiments of concern, saying things like, "'today was a very hard day for the jury'; 'the photos got *real*, fast for the poor jurors; y'all, these jurors, man…'" while reminding her audience, we were just regular people who did not volunteer for this difficult undertaking. Further noting that none of us were in a profession like crime scene investigation *because* we chose not to be, and probably for reasons such as having zero interest in grisly homicides. Although I was unaware of this at the time, I feel obliged to recognize that her compassion is still very much appreciated. As it turns out, we had a shared worry that day. She told her alibiers, "One juror, in particular, stood out to me. She was fidgeting in her chair and kept her hands on her face. At one point she asked for a Kleenex. I thought she was going to wipe her eyes, but instead she dabbed beads of sweat from her forehead." I remember this very clearly. We sat near each other. My maternal instinct left me wanting to do something—anything—especially when she hastily reached toward our candy dish then grabbed, emptied, and placed it in her lap—just in case.

I felt for those who struggled through Dr. Riemer's testimony. It was very unsettling, and depending on our individual experience, could have a lasting emotional impact. I recently had the opportunity to meet with a fellow juror turned author. Tom Evans served on the jury for *Idaho vs. Lori Vallow Daybell*. He mentioned court officials had concerns the jurors' mental health could be impacted by their service, so they extended an offer to pay for counselling services should the need arise. He was aware of a few who welcomed the opportunity, as the Vallow Daybell case, much like ours, was gruesome. The autopsy photos of Lori's children—her victims—Tylee Ryan (16) and JJ Vallow (7) were equally, if not exceedingly more, graphic. Tom mentioned when they were waiting to enter the courtroom for the medical examiner's testimony, the bailiff walked down the line handing out vomit bags. We would have welcomed this safeguard but made it through—and with only one near miss. Tom also let me know they, too, managed to survive without incident.

Nothing could prepare me for the autopsy photographs. Those who followed the Murdaugh case closely will not be shocked to learn the admittance of these gruesome images came with an unusual complexity. When evaluating the overall relevance and admissibility of such supporting evidence, the Federal Rules of Evidence (FRE) dictate it first must be determined that, "The probative value needs to substantially outweigh their prejudicial impact." Obviously, in the case of *SC vs. Richard Alexander Murdaugh*, the former was agreed upon by both sides, but it did not come without some shock value especially to Dr. Riemer and former Attorney General, Charlie Condon:

Dr. Riemer: In my 20+ years of experience, trial judges frequently do not allow gruesome autopsy photos to be shown at all during trial because of the intense emotions they elicit which are believed to prejudice the jury against the defendant. In this case, Judge Newman allowed the photos which made palpable to the jury the physical brutality of the murders.

Charlie Condon [as posted on X]: It is very unusual to have graphic color autopsy photos shown to jurors. The defense is not objecting because it helps make their argument believable. Alex Murdaugh would never gruesomely murder Maggie and Paul because of money troubles. The state offers these photos to show manner and severity of crimes.

At the time, I was unaware something so ubiquitous, like photographs, could potentially influence a jury—especially if they are colorized. Guy expounds on the sentiments expressed by Riemer and Condon remarking, "Color photographs contain more detail and can appear more graphic than black and white versions, and such evidence when viewed in full color is undoubtedly going to be more emotive than when seen in black and white. As a result, jurors can feel a heightened response of horror and disgust." To us, it would not have mattered if the photos applied the brightest Instagram filter; what was done to Maggie and Paul was heinous.

I, for one, think it is very important for juries to see the victims' sustained injuries because they *may* offer a glimpse into the defendant's guilt and/or mentality during the alleged crime. The saying "There's a fine line between love and hate" is one most people have heard a time or two or ten. Likewise, true crime docuseries have taught viewers the same is true for the exceedingly thin line which separates overkill from a crime of passion. Validating this as truth, retired homicide detective Richard Pickett maintains, "The presence of overkill suggests a crime of passion and that in 99% of overkill cases, the perpetrator knows the victim." From the moment I learned and saw what was done to Maggie, my thought was, crime of passion. Then when all testimony had concluded, I discerned he hated her. With Maggie—poor Maggie. *He* did *her* "so bad." Alex hunted his wife like an animal—just like the deer, doves, and feral hogs at Moselle. He circled the mother of his children like a shark circling its prey. He played with her. Each of the five shots seemed personal: one in her torso, another in the upper abdomen, a third in her thigh, then a fourth in the wrist, and for his fifth shot—her head—boring a wound so big he told the 911 operator, "I can see a hole in her head." What was done to Paul was also horrendous, but I do not think Alex planned to "debrain" his son. It is my belief, he intended for his first shot to be the only one. He fired once, then became startled and panicked that Paul remained upright and staggering, so he fired a second time, causing catastrophic damage.

Something distinctive in this case as Alex "confessed" several times on the stand. When Creighton asked Alex about the murders, his mouth was saying No, but his head was nodding up and down saying Yes. Something I did not fully recognize as an admission of guilt, at the time, was discussed on the podcast *Hidden True Crime* which reminded listeners that Alex's own words were not just deflection, but a confession:

"Whoever did that hated Paul Murdaugh."
"Whoever did this had a lot of anger in their heart."
"Whoever did this had been planning it a long time."
"I believe the boat wreck is the reason why Paul and Maggie were killed."

They explain further that the Murdaugh family had so many secrets dating back generations. After the boat crash, their secrets began revealing themselves like a slow drip, and before too long, the levee was breached. Dr. John maintains:

He basically just told us why he killed them. He's right the boat wreck is the reason, but it's not a vigilante—it's him because the boat crash is the unraveling of the Murdaugh Dynasty, and that's what he wants to protect at all costs... I don't think it's accurate they were doing great as a couple. I think that they were probably struggling; she was spending most of her time at Edisto, so I think it is possible he was mad at Maggie for rejecting him and for trying to decipher their financials...I think he blamed Maggie for being an inadequate mother and for her failure to really reign in Paul.

Considering the totality of the prosecution's case and Alex's time on the witness stand, we gained some insight into what rage started this shooting spree, but we will never claim to understand it.

It was less disturbing to see Maggie and Paul amid the setting of a frenetic, fluid crime scene with the red and blue lights of emergency vehicles piercing the darkness and a soundtrack of distressed dogs and police scanners invading the tranquility of rural Islandton. Examining a bustling crime scene through an often unsteady and out-of-focus lapel camera made it easy to look at others in the frame. Instead of gawking at Maggie and Paul's blood-soaked clothes and bullet-ravaged bodies lying prostrate on the hard ground—vulnerable to a gathering storm and leering eyes—some family, some friends, but mostly strangers. However, seeing their bodies under the florescent lighting of a cold, sterile pathologist's laboratory disturbed me more than I ever imagined it would. There was an immense feeling of finality in the autopsy photos which just wasn't present in Daniel Greene's body camera footage. It was not only the resolute finality that accompanied their death, but the swirling, widening gyre of inquiries that followed. Consequently, the center could not hold, and things fell apart, collapsing the family's generational power, culminating in the exposure of Alex's decades of financial scheming and systematic theft.

Dr. Riemer explained the victims' injuries in graphic detail, not because of a covert agenda designed to further vilify the defendant. She was simply speaking the facts as she evaluated them at autopsy. I tried many times to explain, in reasonable necessity, what we saw; however, it was impossible to describe such savagery while remaining deferential to Maggie, Paul, and their surviving family. Therefore, I have chosen to rely upon Dr. Riemer's own testimony:

Maggie first suffered a gunshot wound to her left breast, and the bullet travelled upward to the left side of her face. She had projectiles, ammunition going through her left kidney. You can imagine that was a very painful wound and could have caused her to fold over in pain. The fatal shot went into and out of her chest and into her face basically destroying her brain . . . Paul's brain was blown out the back of his head and the organ arrived at the morgue in a separate bucket . . . the entry wound was below the 22-year-old's left ear and the buckshot pellets blew out of the top of the back of his head.

The most difficult days were ones when the focus was on his victims, not Alex or the madness that encircled him. Painful testimony like Dr. Riemer's felt isolating. Facing these distressing exhibits that were under court seal and intended for our eyes only, made the prohibition on discussing the case with each other torturous. It felt as if our head and heart were engaged in battle, to what end, I did not know. We saw things that could not be unseen; our minds held those grisly images in a vise and refused to release them. Emotionally we wrestled with understanding what kind of intense feelings could evoke such devastation *and* from a man whose duty, as a husband and father, was to love and protect the very two he brutally executed.

After hours of hearing and seeing the entirety of the destruction Alex inflicted on two people he claimed to love, the distress among us was palpable. It was obvious we wanted to talk about it. However, under our legal oath, to which we always closely adhered, we managed to muddle through the uneasiness. It did not take long for us to bond as a group, so it was seldom difficult to pick up on non-verbal cues about how each of us was feeling. We just let intuition be our guide and worked to lift each other up as best we could. Many jurors prayed together, others offered compassionate hugs, while a few just preferred to sit quietly by the window and people watch.

Having heard—and now seen—the carnage that remained of two once vibrant people, Dr. Riemer's testimony remained powerful. Of course, none of us knew the victims, or we would have been dismissed, but as compassionate humans it was impossible not to feel absolutely broken. Maggie and Paul, two people cherished by family and friends, were ambushed in the very place they should have felt most safe and at the hands of a person they would least suspect. They did not have the opportunity to defend themselves because there was *never* a sense of danger. In addition, this testimony evoked our empathy, as each of us has a Maggie and a Paul which made the crime feel personal. Before Maggie was a murder victim, she was the youngest of two daughters born to Kennedy and Terry Branstetter; she was Marian's little sister, a Kappa Delta soror, friend and mother. Paul was Maggie's baby, Buster's brother, a nephew, and treasured friend.

Trial analysts often asked reporters in the courtroom, "Could you tell what the jury was thinking?" On the days Dr. Riemer testified, that was the first question they asked. I feel this reflected their own visual discomfort with the images her testimony elicited, such observations included, but are not limited to the following:

Dr. Riemer (*Personal Communication*): "I recall seeing looks of shock and horror on the part of some jurors when autopsy photos were being shown."

Gigi McKelvey (*Pretty Lies and Alibis*): "The jury was very deeply disturbed by the pathologist's testimony. Each seemed to have their own reaction. A few were stoic, others diverted their eyes, faces got red. Judge Newman was very observant of the jury and took a break after showing the photos of inside Paul's skull."

Michael Dewitt (*Greenville News*): "During this grue-some, morbid testimony, which included autopsy pho-tos sealed by the court from the public, one female juror clutched her mouth and appeared shaken."

Charlie Condon: "There were several jurors who couldn't watch or look at the photos of Paul and one broke down in tears."

I was shocked and horrified, but I did not turn away. Their injuries were incomprehensible, like the manifestation of a terri-ble nightmare. This was proof, now more than ever, that we had a job to do. I am in no way criticizing my fellow jurors if they turned away or peeped through a facepalm. We were ordinary citizens, who brought an array of experiences to the jury box—some of which are heartbreaking and others heartwarming. We were thrust into this horrendous family tragedy and under oath to mete out justice for Maggie and Paul.

During her testimony, Dr. Riemer exhibited the inherent con-fidence and flawless aplomb, once a prerequisite for any woman in a male-dominated field. It is only recently that female forensic pathologists outnumber the males. *CareerExplorer* cites the di-vide as "61% female and 39% male." Finding herself *twice* caught in the crosshairs of Dick Harpootlian's dogged questioning, Dr. Riemer maintained unbelievable resilience. One that I most as-suredly could *never* muster. He grew angrier and louder each time she would double, even triple down with scientific fact. His desperate and ludicrous campaign to discredit her never gained the momentum he desired.

You may recall, their first tussle happened just after losing two jurors to Covid, so we were wearing masks which veiled our giggles. Both times Dr. Riemer was cross-examined it played out like the legendary cinematic sword fight between The Black Knight and King Arthur (*Monty Python and The Holy Grail*). Harpootlian would lob a preposterous hypothetical at her, then she would slice it with scientific precision. Like the Black Knight, who immediately loses an appendage, Dick lets his hubris do the talking and says, "Tis but a scratch." He tried a second time. She thwacked; he rallied quipping, "Tis but a flesh wound." The Black Knight, now a limbless, stump of a man, called for a draw. Harpootlian had the same goal in mind when he pressed Dr. Riemer to say, "An opinion is just an opinion." He may have felt victorious thinking she knuckled-under; however, the reality is she grew weary and tossed him a participation ribbon.

As we moved into the last days of the trial, she was called back to be a rebuttal witness. When Dick stood to approach the lectern, my heart ached for her. I was hoping they would pass the cross to Jim. However, Harpootlian's ego must have been clamoring for a rematch. We were astonished he recycled the losing playbook from two weeks prior. This included familiar greatest hits like: attack her assessment techniques ("more pictures should have been taken; where are your notes?"); attack her procedures (why did you not shave his head; why did you not x-ray his brain?); attack and yell about everything ("answer the question; you go off on tangents; scream about the gunshot wound book;

rage about contact wounds). By the time Dr. Riemer left the witness stand for the last time, the final score of their courtroom beatdown was 2-Love.

Countless professionals have experienced having their qualifications called into question by someone who is unqualified to do so. However, most have not experienced it on the world's stage like Dr. Riemer. We should all strive to have a modicum of her restraint. It was exceptionally painful watching Harpootlian's attempted demolition of a brilliant pathologist. I found myself biting my tongue, as not to shout and be held in contempt. I silently repeated, "You better stop." I knew prayer was my only hope of enduring that torture. Within a few minutes, Dick uttered the phrase I loved to hear most from his mouth, "I have no further questions, your honor."

Special Agent Peter Rudofski: Agent Rudofski took the stand on day 20 as the state's final witness and delivered bombshell testimony. Using a multitude of data sources, he assembled a comprehensive timeline. It was happenstance his testimony was able to come together the way it did, as a sizeable portion of his report was constructed from OnStar data. In March of 2022, General Motors (GM) declared there were no findings linked to Murdaugh's Suburban. We were made aware that this was new information which was previously believed unavailable. Before testimony began, Creighton Waters confirmed the origins of this newly acquired information stating, "During the course of this trial (GM) called and said, oh wait, we found something?" This was baffling as it was happening. How did a big corporation drop the ball or was there some payoff? Given how damaging this was to Alex's timeline, I was confused by Harpootlian's compliance. We sat waiting for the melee to begin, alas it did not. Maybe it was sent over at the last minute to prevent a public relations nightmare. On her podcast, Gigi McKelvey introduced his testimony by telling listeners, "I totally think somebody that works at GM was watching the trial, and they are saying we don't comply with subpoenas—get this stuff to them."

I was slack-jawed the entire time he was on the witness stand. We leaned forward, elbows on knees, fastened to every word, and listened intently as he unveiled fresh details of Alex's movements on that June day, making mental notes of discrepancies from his law enforcement interviews. Reporters from *The State* described this seismic testimony as one which "offered the world a microscopic and intimate look at June 7, 2021. He served up a timeline consisting of cellphone records, text messages and location data from Paul and Maggie's phone. OnStar data showed the exact times and car speeds reached between Moselle and his parents' and the return." We learned the Suburban slowed down leaving Moselle—in the *exact* location where Maggie's phone would be located the following day with speed variations reaching 80 mph. Law enforcement said they never drive beyond the posted speed limit of 55 mph because it is a safety hazard with potholes and deer.

Another data point which played over-and-over in my mind, throughout the rest of trial, was the timestamp between arriving at the murder scene and placing the call to 911, on which he asserted to have taken the pulses of both Paul and Maggie, stating, "I... I... I already touched them trying to get... uhm, to see if they were breathing." Agent Rudofski debunked Alex's claim when he revealed he was only at the kennels for twenty seconds before calling emergency services. I will say, on cross-examination, I did have pause to rethink this timeframe as we sat in a deafeningly silent courtroom when Phillip Barber used his phone's timer to illustrate "twenty seconds." However, I maintain even with the stealth and speed of a jaguar this is an impossible feat. Then, in a made for television "Perry Mason Moment" the prosecution rested their case.

I: CHARACTER WITNESSES:

The state's expert witnesses brought clarity and understanding to the more nuanced aspects of this complex case, while the personal ones helped us to not lose sight of our purpose—getting justice for Maggie and Paul, while reminding us, we were not chosen to convict a confessed thief. The witnesses who embodied the emotional intricacies of this murder trial—two employees and one family member—Shelley Smith, Blanca Simpson, and Marian Proctor revealed a portrait of deep devotion. It is unarguable that their testimony was instrumental in the conviction of Richard Alexander Murdaugh, illustrating the very essence of senior rights advocate, Maggie Kuhn's instruction to, "Speak your truth, even if your voice shakes."

Ms. Shelley Smith: Still, almost two years later, just thinking about this testimony makes me feel misty-eyed. Shelley Smith, a caretaker for ailing Murdaugh matriarch Ms. Libby, took the stand with a fear as palpable as her abiding loyalty and affection for the family.

As a witness, she was central to the prosecution's timeline, a key to Alex's "iron-clad" alibi, and pivotal in discerning the factual alibi from the fictional one. I suspected Ms. Shelley would give us at least a sliver of light to better understand the truth behind what transpired at the kennels. I was wrong; we were blinded by the light of her testimony.

Through tears, she recounted that in the evening hours of June 7, 2021, Alex came over to check on his mother. He strolled in, stayed briefly, and after twenty minutes, flitted out. By the time she took the stand, we had heard the "alibi" many times; however, Ms. Shelley brought with her some intriguing new details. When first questioned by investigators, she stated the truth in—he was there about twenty minutes. However, after the murders, Alex told her he had stayed there 30-40 minutes. Knowing her financial vulnerability, he attempted to buy her loyalty, by first offering to pay for her wedding, then trying to entice her with promises of getting her a higher paying job at the school where she worked food service. Alex essentially threatened her livelihood for telling the truth, while her freedom could be risked for lying to law enforcement and obstructing justice, as he intimated was his preference. Alex Murdaugh underestimated the strength Ms. Shelley possessed as she refused to become another victim tangled in this web of deceit. Her love for the Murdaughs was apparent in every tear she shed. Her loyalty to the family was overt in her hesitation to recount the actual events of that evening and in the aftermath of the tragedy.

I can't imagine that any reasonable person could deem Ms. Shelley an unreliable witness, but since it seems every cause has a hater, Agent Rudofski corroborated and vindicated her recollection of events. His data established he was there just long enough to check-in so he could check-off "manufacture alibi" from his murder to do list. Likewise, she also shared details of Alex's suspicious behavior in the days following the murders. He came to the house early in the morning and went upstairs carrying something blue that resembled a tarp or jacket. A search warrant later found an oversized blue raincoat with "gunshot residue particles across the interior and exterior of the coat."

Blanca: Shelley Smith delivered powerful testimony, so I had every reason to believe the same about Blanca. Working in the Murdaugh home(s) provided them a familiarity that Alex likely never considered, so it was not surprising how quickly they detected even the most nuanced changes in his behavior and habits.

When Blanca took the stand, John Meadors did an amazing job of giving Blanca ample time to discuss her family, accomplishments, and relationship with the Murdaughs. Gaining an understanding of who she was prior to becoming a confidante to Maggie and the Murdaugh's housekeeper. She established herself as a smart, accomplished woman, a veteran, a leader who would provide us with astute insight about the weeks/days leading up to the murders, as well as Maggie's financial concerns about the impending boat case for which she felt Alex was withholding information. YouTube legal sensation Emily D. Baker provides real-time commentary while streaming high profile cases for her followers; she referred to her testimony as "a fount of damaging information" and as "the witness who could turn everything around in the case"

Blanca, like Shelley Smith, was a deeply loyal employee which automatically suggests a power differential and a threat to their financial security. Of this relationship, Journalist Liz Farrell, highlighted how unusual it was to see "a paid employee of the Murdaughs speak out in a way that was against the narrative of the family," and continued with kudos because Blanca (and Shelley Smith) stuck to personal values, told the truth, and refused to obstruct justice.

Alex, once again, attempted the ole choreograph a fact gambit. With Blanca it came months later after an unnerving *third* interview with lead detective David Owen, the one where Alex learned he remained in the investigative circle. Anxious and pacing in the living room, he told Blanca, "I have a bad feeling," then indicated to her that he was wearing a Vineyard Vines shirt on the day of the murder, which was categorically false. Blanca expressed zero doubt when describing how, that morning, she adjusted the collar on a sea-foam colored polo style shirt—which she never saw again. She recalled feeling stunned and wondered if that was how *he wanted* her to answer the question, if asked. Blanca testified about pooled water in the bathroom, a wet towel on the closet floor, and a T-shirt which had fallen from an upper shelf. She clarified things I had not even questioned, none more chilling than the revelation Maggie wanted to stay at Edisto that evening. But Alex wanted her home because his father's health was rapidly declining; he lured his wife to Moselle and used his dying father as bait.

Marian Proctor: I still get an aching in my soul when I think of the heartbreaking testimony given by Maggie's only sibling, Marian Proctor. She confirmed what Blanca had said earlier—Maggie was not supposed to be at Moselle that night and testified to Alex's state of mind following the murders. She let the world know that while the family and law firm remained frightened the perpetrators may return, his number one priority was clearing Paul's name. Internally she questioned his priorities. Alex's main goal should have been finding the killer and protecting Buster. I agree wholeheartedly with prosecutor David Fernandez, who considered her among the most powerful witnesses noting, "She was a true victim, and I think the jury got that. The juxtaposition between herself and Alex is that she genuinely was torn apart by what happened. It was true emotions from her. Your heart broke; I was horribly upset hearing her testimony." We felt every moment of her pain as she relived June 7, 2021, and its aftermath. Marian's time on the stand brought forth startling evidence that was either muddied or absent in previous testimony—a consciousness and admission of guilt directly from the culprit's lips. She recounted speaking privately with Alex asking if he knew who might be responsible. In a cryptic reply he said, "I don't know who could have done this, but whoever it was had been thinking about it a really long time." Creighton Waters asked if she felt that was an odd reply, and she said, "I just didn't know what that meant." I think it was a coy admission of guilt, for which there were many, as we'd learn throughout trial. Just thinking of this statement, over a year later, I find myself equally as chilled and speechless as I was on the day of her testimony.

Shelley, Blanca, and Marian were extraordinary witnesses. They each contributed something unique and central to this 2,000-piece puzzle we were building. Without their testimony, we would have very little information about Alex's state of mind in the immediate aftermath of the murders, as well as the months which followed—all which ultimately helped us to arrive at our *unanimous* verdict of guilty.

III: MOST VALUABLE PLAYERS:

No discussion of the witnesses and their contribution to this trial would be complete without three silent witnesses— Paul, Bubba, and Cash. The crime fighting trio of a little detective, a mischievous labrador retriever and a playful puppy colluded to bring forth game changing evidence.

Bubba: Science tells us that dogs can sense things long before humans know danger is lurking, and we will never know the depth of Bubba's intuition on June 7, 2021. What prompted him to go on a chicken chase that night? Was it a case of the evening zoomies? Was the chicken just feeling cocky and decided a sneak attack would be fun? Regardless, had he not returned to the kennels eager and excited to flaunt his prized poultry, Alex's big lie may have never been exposed.

Because Bubba was locked in his kennel, he could not intervene physically, but this good boy had a plan B—chase that pesky chicken. The bite on Cash's tail and Bubba's stunt provided the state their *coup de grâce*. Alex had no choice but to confess that he lied about being at the kennels.

Shortly after the verdict, WLTX out of Columbia, South Carolina, aired an interview with prosecutor John Meadors who was delivering the news of victory to their MVP witness. In his endearing Southern drawl, he tells the reporter, "I don't think there's a more unconditional love and any other way Bubba could have shown his love for Maggie than what he did that night. I did find it ironic that man's best friend, in this case woman's best friend, became a star witness."

Paul: Each Murdaugh family member or friend who took the witness stand complimented his intelligence, intuition, and immense loyalty. We saw this in his relationship with Rogan and his concern for Cash's tail. Countless legal pundits maintain, "Paul provided key testimony in his own murder trial." Meadors described Paul's recording as "insurance" he had on Alex—just in case the worst happened. No one knew this video existed, and it was very well concealed on his phone which took multiple agencies working together to retrieve it." As it turns out the little detective did not find an important clue, he left behind the biggest clue of all—his phone.

CHAPTER 6:
LAND OF CONFUSION

Only in a high-profile trial featuring Alex Murdaugh as the defendant, could a bomb threat temporarily derail the day's testimony; likewise, only Judge Newman could dismiss a packed courtroom while never wavering from the unflappable control that won hearts across the globe. Whether from home or in the gallery, trial watchers will recall his steady temperance when Mike Atwood, Judge Newman's security chief, approached the bench, just as the morning's third witness was being sworn in for testimony. Judge Newman leaned across his clerk to meet Atwood's hushed tone, never offering any sign of alarm. He remained measured, as if he were just told something innocuous like, "Your wife needs to leave for an appointment, and you have the keys." I don't recall being particularly concerned by their exchange. Judge Newman's voice steady, he excused us. The gallery rose then we began our exit. As soon as the doors closed behind us, it became very clear—this was not an early lunch break. There was an urgent purpose and substance to the hasty excusal.

It was day thirteen of Alex Murdaugh's double murder trial. We had long since settled into our daily routine. We had gotten to know one another quickly, with a fondness that was growing daily. We knew the court staff and bailiffs by name and when to expect a stretch break or brief recess.

February 8, 2023, began and ended just the same as the preceding twelve had and as the proceeding fifteen would. It's what happened in the middle that was extraordinary. We gathered at the designated parking lot, took our short ride to the courthouse, then chitchatted over coffee and light breakfast fare. Once the defense and prosecution had hammered out the day's housekeeping details, Judge Newman would cue the bailiff that he was ready for us, by sunnily proclaiming "bring the jury" (something I would learn months later). We lined up according to our specified seat in the jury box, then walked in before a crowd which was standing out of deference and staring out of curiosity for the twelve charged with deciding the fate of the legal scion.

The day's first witness was Megan Fletcher from SLED who reviewed the gunshot residue (GSR) test results. She declared particles were found on his shirt, shorts, and hand, along with one particle on the seatbelt of his SUV, and a startling amount of GSR was identified both on the inside and outside of the now infamous "blue tarp/blue rain poncho" that Ms. Shelley earlier testified she witnessed Alex take into an upstairs room at his mother's house. Investigators would eventually locate something of that description in a second-floor closet.

After Fletcher's tedious, but significant, testimony, Alex's former paralegal of almost ten years, Annette Griswold, took the stand to provide important insight into her former employer. She described his presence at work as being much like that of the tornadic *Looney Tunes* character Taz, so much so she jokingly referred to him as the Tasmanian devil. Annette continued by mentioning that despite his chaotic nature, she considered Alex intelligent and someone she once respected and admired. Griswold recalled observing grim changes in his persona after the boat crash, which unbeknownst to everyone, except Alex, posed a direct threat to the family legacy of wealth and power, chipping away at it daily bit-by-bit. Annette, like countless others, thought she knew him. Telling her story of finding a check for lost funds, she revealed, "I was hurt. I was angry. I was beside myself, and I was a bit enraged too." The wealthy, yet humble, fun-loving, family man that Alex Murdaugh portrayed himself to be, proved a façade—a cunning masquerade—for someone who would be revealed, in a very public manner, as nothing more than the wolf of Hampton County.

After Annette's heartrending testimony, Judge Newman paused proceedings, then excused us. We stood and filed out of the same side doors that we entered and exited through multiple times a day. I don't recall feeling confused or worried; everything happened so quickly. If I thought anything, it would be that maybe I zoned out and missed a sidebar, since those often resulted in Judge Newman sending us to our room(s) for a time out. Once those doors closed behind us, a bailiff began shouting, "Let's Go; let's go. Grab your stuff and hurry!" At that point, I realized there was measured purpose in our dismissal—this was *not* a drill. Whatever was going on had to be serious and potentially dangerous for everyone in the Colleton County Courthouse. What in the world was happening? Did some fool catch the office microwave on fire? Was there a creature in the ceiling who set off smoke signals while chewing through some wires?

After bounding down the stairs and finally making it outdoors, we were divided evenly into two groups of nine, as it would be a few days yet before Covid would run rampant through the jury box. We boarded the same Blackout vans that took us to and from the courthouse every morning and every evening. Once the vehicle began moving, the bailiff finally revealed what was happening, saying, an unknown person (at the time) called to say, "There was a bomb in the judge's chambers." I am in no way criticizing the delay in telling us what was going on. It's understandable they did not want to create undue hysteria that could potentially make for a dangerous evacuation. Clearly, our safety was of paramount concern to court staff and law enforcement, which was, and still is, very much appreciated.

Our transport vehicles, along with those carrying court officials, were led to safety by a police escort at the helm and one at the rear. We sheltered at the Colleton County School District Office, a location so secure, Captain Chapman remarked, "It was so secure that we had to remind some of our personnel during transfer where it was." We remained in one room, while Judge Newman, his wife, and law clerk, Gabby, along with several courthouse staff remained separate from us in another room down the hall. Knowing many of our loved ones were likely tuned in to watch the trial, or otherwise might soon learn of the evacuation, the bailiff offered his phone to anyone who wanted to check-in with family. I knew my mom had to be watching. She watched every single hour of it—every single day. I quickly took him up on the offer and so did several other jurors. There was no doubt in my mind she was edging quickly toward a code red on the worried Mom scale by this point. The call connected; it rang and rang, so I tried my dad. He answered, letting me know the two of them were in Beaufort. They had no idea the courthouse had to suddenly be vacated, but were, nonetheless, grateful I phoned to let them know I was safe.

It was evident court officials had an emergency preparedness plan which proved flawless from evacuation to reentry. Paramedics were even in place just in case a need arose. It is my guess this may be necessary for a medical emergency or fire. I am sure a bomb threat was not on their trial of the century bingo card. Captain Jason Chapman was asked about how seamlessly things moved throughout the duration of the trial and during the bomb threat, saying, "It ran so smooth mainly because of months of preparation and these guys (pointing to Detectives Laura Rutland and Daniel Greene). We met once a week for two months. We wanted it run and practiced, so when it was time for the trial to start, we didn't have any flaws."

If the courthouse team was concerned, none of us could tell. Once we were all situated in our temporary jury room, the clerk and her deputy sprang into action and took our lunch order. Among ourselves we asked, who in the world would do such a thing? Why? A bomb threat—I thought those were just for prank callers of the nineteen eighties and had faded into the past with *69 and caller ID.

By now, the world over knows if Alex Murdaugh's mouth is moving, he is lying in some capacity or another. However, he has spoken factually about one thing—people "yip yap!" The bomb threat was no different, and social media was there for it:

ArtTherapy73: Alex Murdaugh calling in his own bomb threat to interrupt testimony regarding the mountain of evidence against him, wouldn›t surprise me in the least.

Oucrimsongirl: I don't believe in coincidences, and I would not put it past Alex Murdaugh to orchestrate a bomb threat.

Swavey_orlando: LOL a bomb threat at the Alex Murdaugh trial!?! They doin whatever to cause a mistrial.

Staceybeth69: Question—Does Cousin Eddie have anything to do with this bomb threat?!?

Despite X users having a little fun with the situation, if there had been validity to the phone call, this could have been a dire situation. The vigilance of emergency personnel ensured our safe transfer and the courthouse's flawless evacuation. Anne Emerson inquired of Rutland, Greene, and Chapman, how they were able to relocate priority persons, keep all attendees safe, and release a statement soon thereafter. Chapman describes the process:

> We pretty much had the entire property evacuated in about five minutes. After evac, we returned to the law enforcement trailer, then brought in representatives from the local phone company, county IT, SLED, and the Sheriff's office . . . The detectives began working on trying to get back to the source. Detective Rutland continues, there were like two or three of us on the phone, each talking to a different analyst. Then we just kind of combined everything that we got, and SLED agents were able to pinpoint where the phone call was coming from. We all worked together and within six hours we had it.

Looking back at Judge Newman's initial announcement of, "Ladies and gentlemen, we have to evacuate the building and will be in recess until we discover what's going on" the defendant had an authentic look of confusion. It seemed in line with the rest of the courtroom and millions of trial watchers worldwide. However, when he overheard Doug, the defense's AV tech, telling Jim Griffin the evacuation was because of a bomb threat, Alex offered up a smirk which would be heard round the world, igniting a social media tinderbox of gossip, rumor, and innuendo. Understandably so, it reeked of a classic Murdaugh deflection strategy, and social media agreed. About two weeks after the bomb threat, users could not wait to comment on a post by reporter Liz Farrell. She shared a reel from the trial, captioned, "Memories: The smirk when Alex Murdaugh was told about the bomb threat":

Jess_Isnt_Jaded: That's an, "I can't believe it worked" expression if I've ever seen one.

Giuseppe_jimmy: Tells the tale doesn't it?

JessicaRameyGil: Body Language. Is oft. Involuntary.

TylerHartigan: I heard they're investigating the caller. They've tracked it back to a man named Nick Charcootlian.

Blue_Freedom: I don't know anything about this trial, but anyone that enjoys hearing court is interrupted due to a bomb threat is a sociopath.

In the ensuing weeks, we would finally learn who was responsible for bringing the trial of the century to a three-hour grinding halt. However, I am not sure we will ever know what motivated the caller, an inmate being held at the Ridgeland Correctional Institute. Perhaps he just wanted an increase in the 30 years he was already serving for a slew of charges. Investigators, well over a year later, still contend there is no discernable link between the caller and Murdaugh. It is not the detectives I doubt—it's Alex. I would not be surprised to learn that a certain inmate found a Thank You basket full of Honey Buns and Beef Sticks when he arrived in his new cell at the Broad River Secure Facility in Columbia, South Carolina. "X" user Alicia Roberts implied the two were in cahoots and succinctly stated what millions were thinking, "Boy I tell ya, they were right! Every time Alex is in the hot seat, something happens. This time, a bomb threat at the courthouse!"

Just as coolly as Judge Newman adjourned the court a few hours prior, he convened the trial day without any mention of the disruption. Justice may have been delayed by a few hours that February afternoon, but it would not end as a case of justice denied.

CHAPTER 7:
HOUSE OF THE RISING SUN

For six weeks, we looked at photos, bodycam video, drone footage, and maps of the Murdaugh's vast hunting estate. These visuals helped each of us create a unique image of the expanse between the kennels and house. As the distance between the two, or rather lack thereof, was central to every iteration of his alibi. However, understanding maps is not in everyone's wheelhouse. In fact, some of the smartest people I know would never make it to work if it meant they had to use a roadmap. Until the jury visit, we had a varying degree of understanding and even more misunderstandings, of the actual spread which separated the family home from the crime scene. Thankfully, for us, yet probably to the chagrin of the defense, because of seeing it for ourselves, we did not have to engage in geography wars during deliberation.

Once the evidence was presented and both sides rested, Judge Newman announced we would be going on a site visit to Moselle. Back in the jury room we enjoyed a good laugh, as someone interjected, "That must be the big surprise our driver was teasing about this morning? So, I guess this means we are not getting a pizza party after all!" This field trip did not come as a total shock. I remember Harpootlian mentioned something about it during opening statements but never gave it another thought. Our impending visit to Moselle just added to the media frenzy, both at the courthouse and in cyberspace. Journalists and analysts were aflutter, conjecturing about which side stood to benefit the most from the jury visit. Dick commented to reporters, "You just can't really appreciate the spatial issues without really seeing them." Jury consultant, Natalie Gordon, similarly noted these visits can be a sensory experience which "can empower jurors to see for themselves and feel personally involved, and it sometimes can prove more powerful than witness testimony." The insights of both Harpootlian and Gordon were letter-perfect; however, as you know, the defense's request did not yield the results they had hoped.

Dick and Jim felt a physical orientation of the property would help bolster at least one of their defense theories, yet the prosecution showed trepidation about the site visit. They were concerned about potential jury misinterpretation, due to the evolution of the landscape over the twenty months Moselle sat abandoned. Valerie Bauerlein, pool reporter for the jury site visit, provided this firsthand account of one such significant change, "Standing near where Maggie's body fell with my back turned to the shed, I could barely make out the tin roof of the main house over the top of the tree line, due to the stand of pine trees which have grown an estimated two feet or so since the night of the homicides." I can see how a person who did not take this natural thickening into consideration might have clouded judgement when piecing together the events of June 7, 2021. After all, such growth could buffer the sound of gunfire at the Moselle of 2023, but not so much on the night of the murders. It also stands to reason that dense tree coverage might serve as an optical allusion, of sorts, giving the impression there is a greater distance between the two locations. Both of which would have increased the believability of his original lalibi—the one where he was napping in the AC and playing on his phone. In this case, the walls of the Murdaugh home very well could have silenced the salvo of gunfire at the kennels. However, based on the timeline details of his final alibi—the one where Alex rescued the chicken then left to go back to the house—would have placed him outside at the time of the murders where seven gunshots would have reverberated through the noiseless summer evening.

Before boarding our transport vans, Judge Newman took an opportunity to recap a few housekeeping details. First and foremost, there was not to be any talking among us or other personnel. Should questions arise, we were only to ask him. Next, he repeated, the visit was limited to exterior areas (save for the feed room). He concluded by addressing the prosecution's unease, saying, "It has been a year and a half or more since June 7, 2021, when the alleged crime occurred. Things have most likely changed. We are in a different season of the year." This was an excellent reminder for the Lowcountry natives among us, as around here, it is not uncommon for the calendar season to conflict with outside temperatures.

We would depart the courthouse shortly after 9:00 a.m. Leading the caravan to Moselle was Judge Newman who rode in a dark-colored truck driven by Captain Jason Chapman and behind us was what Bauerlein referred to as a "phalanx of security vehicles and court personnel." The drive time for the twenty-two-mile excursion was estimated to take about thirty minutes. It certainly felt like much longer than that; we shared a laugh or two about how it felt like we were leaving civilization. I expected one of the guys to begin a light-hearted rallying call of "Mr. Bill, can we please make a pit stop; it's an emergency" or "Are we there yet?" Having lived in the Lowcountry for so long, I often—too often—take its rich, unique beauty for granted. However, there were a few times on our drive, I was rapt in the solemnity of what we were about to experience. It was then I allowed my mind to wander as I drank in the splendor of this place, I am lucky enough to call home. Unspoiled highways are uncommon in our area which otherwise seems to boast a new construction project every other week. However, many of the rural roads connecting bustling downtown Walterboro to Moselle are lined by lush trees awash in Spanish moss, which, in places, can be so abundant it canopies the road itself. Lost in prayerful thought watching the silvery green-grey tendrils flutter in the breeze, we, at long last, arrived.

Dismal, grey clouds blanketed the skies during our excursion to the property. The barren trees refused to offer even the tiniest hint spring was imminent; however, the constant beautiful bird-song warbled God's guarantee that rebirth and renewal were near at hand. Visually, it appeared the perfect day to sit by a roaring fire. When we deboarded the vans at the kennels the air was cool. However, the humidity assured us this balmy weather was fleeting. Feeling the sun on our face would have been lovely during our brief outing from the courthouse, but it was ideal for walking the wooded grounds. The cloud coverage kept the temperature just cool enough to keep the swarms of no-see-ums at bay, which ordinarily would have saturated an area like Moselle. Much to our pleasure, and others who would find themselves within nose shot, the slight nip in the air promised we would not return to the jury box still damp with sweat and unpleasantly fragrant.

I started by examining the feed room—the very spot where Alex's murderous rampage began. Looking at the door, I allowed myself an inward snicker amid the grim circumstance. With Dr. Kinsey and Jim's recent courtroom clash fresh on my mind, I could hear his southern drawl, with a skosh of professional exasperation say, "Really, Mr. Griffin it's a cone. The cone... I've already described how the shot pattern works." The ammunition which killed Paul contained slightly north of 50 pellets. After the second shot was fired, those bits spread, and the defects had not faded with time. Seeing for myself how the cone's curved base began toward the top of the door, then rained down into the frame, creating the vertex, gave me goose bumps.

Looking upward, my gaze met the back window. Its spidering glass punctuated with a huge bullet hole shocked me to my core. My mind immediately flashed to the horrific crime scene images we had seen so many times throughout trial. As I turned to exit, walking the same few steps that would be Paul's last, I could see the murder play out in my mind as if it were a short movie narrated by Dr. Kinsey:

The buckshot struck him while he was standing sideways, with his right shoulder facing the door. Blood drops flowed straight down indicating he was standing as he staggered toward the door. The position of the shell casing on the floor of the feed room indicated that most of the gun was inside the feed room when the second shot was fired—at extremely close range which was immediately fatal, and he ceased all voluntary movement.

The shallow room where Paul received the first non-fatal shot was much smaller than it appeared in pictures. In an article on *Buzzfeed News*, fellow juror James McDowell, explained the site visit helped him gain a reasonable understanding of how the catastrophic shot to Paul could have been delivered at an upward angle, "I think if he's looking at Paul and just fired a buckshot—which if you're not firm, it can rock you pretty good. I think he could have been unbalanced and tripped over that threshold which puts him on the ground shooting upwards of where Paul is coming out. This makes sense to me for the angle of the shot." James would later share this perspective during deliberation, which seemed logical to us all. That little feed room had long since been emptied of physical possessions but would forever be brimming with a tale of greed, power, and deceit. A story which will be told for generations.

When people asked what it felt like to visit the crime scene, I struggled trying to find the appropriate word(s). Surreal, that was not accurate, there was nothing unrealistic or dreamlike about seeing where two people were brutally executed by someone they trusted. Macabre, eerie, sinister; nope, those words more appropriately described Alex Murdaugh—the wretch who used his family's sprawling rustic estate as his personal killing field. When I was looking at reports of our visit, I think Valerie Bauerlein described it best, calling it "a heavy place to visit." To hear her say there were only twelve average-sized steps between the final resting spots of Maggie and Paul—mother and son—made my Mama heart ache. Looking back-and-forth between the respective places where their lifeless bodies dropped, Genesis 4:10 came to mind, "And he said, what hast thou done? The voice of thy brother's blood crieth unto me from the ground." This scripture illustrates God's tenets on justice and mercy. For it is understood, blood which is spilled in malicious death must be punished. He will bear the charge of executing justice, while also showing mercy to the sinner. As I stood in the hallowed places where Maggie and Paul transcended their earthly existence, I did not know, quite yet, if they would receive their due justice. But one thing is for certain, the sinner, had already received a pound of mercy, as the crimes for which he was accused were death penalty eligible.

Walking back toward the area where Maggie fell, I began thinking about Dick's hours-long cross-examination of Melinda Worley, specifically that which centered on the quail pin and doghouse, both within feet of where Alex's second victim lain. The defense seemed to cleave to those defects as a means of bolstering their two-shooter theory, which had been refuted many times over. Acquiescing to this *possibility* proved to be Worley's only available exit off Harpootlian's roundabout. I had to see those bullet holes for myself. After close inspection, six weeks of witness testimony illustrated, to me, the shooter was moving. While little to no evidence, showed a scenario where there was more than one perpetrator.

One curious thing I did notice about the doghouse was the like-new toy chicken that had been placed inside. I could only think of two ways it got there. The first, and least likely, explanation was that Dick and Jim planted it as an Easter egg of gratitude to reward us for our six weeks of service. This is just *speculation*, but I would not be surprised if this was a swipe at the prosecution. Afterall Bubba, Maggie's yellow lab, and his prized chicken, ultimately blew apart Alex's alibi and led to the grand jury's indictment. This was the *only* reason Alex's voice was heard, only minutes before Maggie and Paul lost their life, and just like that, the world knew Alex had lied about his whereabouts. He was not on the couch playing on his phone or napping, while trying to escape the heat and humidity of a Lowcountry summer. Bubba's key role was not lost on prosecutor John Meadors who opined the possibility that he sensed something was amiss that prompted him to "get in good trouble" and seize on an innocent fowl. Of the pup's vital testimony, Meadors said, "I don't think there's any other way Bubba could have shown his unconditional love for Maggie than what he did." Concluding his interview by saying,

"It was just so tragic all the way around, just as tragic as it gets, and I did find it ironic that man's best friend, in this case woman's best friend, was a key witness."

After surveying the scene of the murders, our visit concluded at the residence. Knowing a long afternoon of sitting would shortly resume, most of us chose to walk. The distance between the kennels and main house was much shorter than I envisioned. *The Daily Mail* cites it as 366 yards, just over the length of three football fields. The two-dimensional demonstratives shown in court made it seem twice that far.

Making our way to the front of the house, our eyes instantly fell to the bicycle on the front lawn. From the various pictures of Maggie shown during trial, it was obvious she preferred bright, cheerful colors accented in bold patterns. There was no doubt the chartreuse beach cruiser with a large, tattered wicker basket strapped to the rusting handlebars, was the very one many witnesses testified Maggie would ride to the kennels.

The bicycle's saddle and rubber handlebar grips matched, both black and decorated with white tropical flowers. The worn kickstand was in the down position, holding the abandoned bike upright. Maybe Dick and Jim used this as some sort of symbolic prop to garner sympathy for Alex. To me, it looked out of place and left me with an uneasy feeling. To an unknowing bystander, it looked as if the owner parked it there only momentarily, intending to come right back. Were we to believe that Maggie's bike had been standing in situ for almost two full years? Were they trying to gull us into forgetting crucial timeline information? Maggie did not arrive at Moselle until the early evening in where she would share a meal with the person who would soon end her life, as well as that of their son. She did not enjoy a ride around the property earlier that afternoon. Aside from logistics, it did not take a skilled sleuth to notice the obvious. Her bicycle was not weather-beaten from constant exposure to the Lowcountry rains, nor was it covered in the pollen of an early Spring.

The porch was large and spanned the full length of the house. The only furniture which remained were two wooden rocking chairs sitting on either side of a table that resembled a tall milking stool. Carefully placed in its center was a small, dark blue flowerpot. On it was a hand painted snowman against the backdrop of tiny dots representing snow. Printed on the rim, in the impeccable writing of an elementary school teacher, was the name Buster, also accented with spots of snow. I could only assume this was one of Maggie's coveted treasures from her eldest's childhood.

Did Dick and Jim think their cagey set design would shift our focus to Buster and all he had lost, hoping we would find their client innocent. If this was the case, the only thing they showed was how easily they believed we could be manipulated. If Dick and Jim wanted to give Moselle the "the frozen in time" look, the smallest attempt at accuracy would have been a good place to start. The murders happened in the summer; *most* women store their snowman-themed crafts with the Christmas decorations. Secondly, much like Maggie's bicycle, it was not caked in the bright-green grit of a South Carolina snow, referred to by some as pollen.

Moselle's extreme home makeover—the lawyer edition—was made complete with one final potshot at the prosecution. Hanging inside of the upstairs window was a man's shirt. It was almost identical to the one Alex donned in the now infamous "tree video" taken by Paul less than an hour before his murder. This shirt, or absence thereof, became an essential piece of the puzzle. During her testimony, Detective Rutland authenticated the clothes and shoes worn by Alex in that Snapchat recording were not the cargo shorts, white t-shirt and running shoes taken into custody for testing. Likewise, Murdaugh housekeeper Blanca Turrubiate-Simpson substantiated these claims with further elaboration, as she painfully recalled a curious interaction with Alex months after the murders. In reaction to his third interview with lead investigator David Owen, Blanca described Alex asking if she recalled what he was wearing that night, adding, "I got a bad feeling." He tried to plant false memories, asking if she remembered the "Vinny Vines" shirt he was wearing. She told him she only recalled a sea-foam colored *polo* shirt. During direct examination, Blanca explained how she straightened his collar earlier in the day on a shirt that was *not* Vineyard Vines. She told attorney Meadors, "I didn't say anything, but I was kind of thrown back because I don't remember him wearing that shirt that day."

I did not know what to expect from our jury field trip, but I did know instinct would be my guide, making it easy to discern what was significant and what was a manufactured distraction. Afterall, the only context I had for a jury visit to the crime scene was from O.J. Simpson's murder trial. Where prior to his jury visit, defense attorney, Carl Douglas spearheaded a redecoration of his Brentwood estate. Details of his headline making overhaul included, "pictures of him with models were replaced with family members. Large pieces of African art and a Norman Rockwell painting, on loan from Johnnie Cochran's office, now prominently hung on the walls. Conspicuously placed on Simpson's bedside table was a photo of his mother." Douglas claimed this was done so his home would appear "lived-in and standout with its regalness, so jurors would say 'O.J. Simpson would not have risked all of this.'" At the time, I never imagined Dick and Jim would resort to similar shenanigans; nonetheless, it is evident that the respective dream teams, sang from the same song sheet.

"Court Potatoes" of the 1990s will never know how, or even *if*, that visit was instrumental in tipping the scales of justice in Simpson's favor. However, I can definitively say, our personal observations at Moselle helped to solidify the unanimous verdict we would render the following evening. Wherein, for the first time in 87 years, the scales of justice would hang balanced in the Fourteenth Judicial circuit and throughout South Carolina.

Dale Wimbrow's "The Man in the Glass," was framed and hung somewhere in their home; it was eventually sold at the Moselle Estate Auction. The poem eerily foreshadowed Alex's plummet from grace and his ensuing two lifetimes of incarceration, as seen in this haunting stanza, "You may fool the whole world down the pathway of years/And get pats on the back as you pass/But your final reward will be heartache and tears/If you've cheated the man in the glass."

CHAPTER 8:
I STAND ACCUSED

Our constitutional right to "plead the fifth" found its way off its parchment paper of origin and into casual conversation. The phrase is typically used as a "refusal to answer because it might reveal guilt or harm one's self-interest." However, what may be lesser known is its foundation. As fun as it might be to think our forefathers had criminal architects like Alex Murdaugh in mind when penning the constitution is sadly not the reality. What they were considering centered around the inquisitorial methods used by the British Courts of Star (1487- 1681). *Slate* reporter, Dahlia Lithwick explains this brand of truth-seeking was derived from coercing confessions out of the defendant who had "no advanced notice of his accusers, the charges against him, or the evidence amassed." No matter the severity of the accusation, everyone has the right against self-incrimination.

Law professor, Jeffrey Bellin, indicates it is a risky choice any time a defendant chooses to testify on their own behalf; yet the data continually hovers around 50%. He continues by suggesting there may be some benefit to taking the stand in an instance like self-defense; but cautions, there are no guarantees. It famously worked for Kyle Rittenhouse, an Illinois teen who fatally shot two men and injured another, when civil unrest erupted over the police shooting of African American male, Jacob Blake. Through sobs, he was able to convince a jury his actions were in self-defense and was acquitted of all charges. In contrast, the tears did not work for Travis McMichael who was one of the three men convicted of pursuing and killing Ahmaud Arbery, an African American male jogging in a predominately white neighborhood near his home.

Another time counsel may consider this option is if their client is caught in a lie; in this case, attorney Adam Banner suggests, "Take the puncher's chance, and go down swinging. If the damage is done, and there is *no* evidence which could make it more catastrophic—then just hope the jury doesn't hold it against them." Likewise, within the last twelve months, many high- profile defendants—absent a self-defense claim or a bold-faced falsehood that needed justification—gambled and lost. In early November (2023) Charlie Adelson was convicted of first-degree murder, solicitation and conspiracy for the murder of his ex-brother-in-law Dan Markel. His defense—double extortion. I remain undecided if listening to Charlie's rubbish was more painful or equal to Alex's fourteen hours' worth of foolishness. Regarding Charlie Adelson, *Florida Politics* writer Peter Schorsch astutely stated, "I sat down to write a serious recap of Charlie Adelson's murder trial but one can't write seriously about a defense story that on its face is so beyond absurd that Shift+F7 on the word 'absurd' even fails to produce a synonym that captures its irrationality." To that, I pinch my fingers and thumb together, raise them to my lips and toss Mr. Schorsch a chef's kiss, thinking he has surely been working on that ingenious one- liner since the moment Alex Murdaugh *finally* abdicated his throne of lies earlier that year (late February 2023). Likewise, Jennifer Crumbley, the Michigan school shooter mom, suffered a similar outcome. Shannon Smith, her defense attorney, announced during opening statements that her client would take the stand to "tell you about her life, her son ... about the day he became the shooter, and about the day he did something she could have never anticipated or fathomed or predicted." Whether it was her hubris or Smith's that landed the defendant on the witness stand, Crumbley was the ultimate loser. The jury forewoman revealed in a post-verdict interview on the *Today* show, that the defendant's own evidence became the lynchpin and cited her testimony saying, "Once we began deliberating, it became clear she was not a reliable witness. An example was her declaration that she wouldn't have done anything differently leading up to the shooting, despite clear warning signs. This was repeated a lot in the deliberation room. It was upsetting to hear, as there were many small things that could have been done to prevent this. Perhaps defense counsels for Charlie and Jennifer need a refresher course in "to take the stand or not to take the stand." Conventional wisdom of legal analysts agree, attorneys need to consider the following when weighing their client's vulnerability:

Does the defendant have a criminal past? Does their client have any past bad acts which might resurface on the stand?

What is the defendant's overall demeanor? The attorney must be able to *honestly* evaluate their client's affability and credibility.

How is the defendant under pressure? If their client is not able to perform well under the stress of testimony, they may appear nervous, which may be misconstrued for guilt.

In using this assessment model, I *know* there was not one juror who believed it was a good idea for Alex to testify on his own behalf and bet the same was true for all trial watchers, including the most loyal Murdaugh apologists. With lips zipped, locked and the key tossed, he should have just stayed seated betwixt Dick and Jim for the duration of trial. In the weeks leading up to the defense's case-in-chief, we were aware that once the state rested, there was a chance Alex would take the stand. However, it was not something I gave much thought to either way. We were putting the prosecution's puzzle together, piece-by-piece, so there was no chance to focus on the "will he, or won't he?"

This is to say, I certainly would not consider equating his refusal to testify as an admission of guilt. For one, that is a court instruction. Two—lawyer or not—with his slew of other charges, he may not want to say something that could inadvertently damage his legal standing. Murdaugh World stayed true to form, by remaining elusive and non-committal about the possibility their client may testify on his own behalf. Mutters among media got louder, while Dick and Jim got wilier, filing an absurd "just in case" motion that would limit the scope of cross-examination to only the murder charges. Concerning their ridiculous request, Judge Newman diplomatically replied, "For the court to issue some blanket order limiting the extent of cross-examination is unheard of to me." Despite this, Dick and Jim decided to tee up their Hail Mary and go whole hog on a witness who would ultimately devastate their case; not unlike the feral hogs who ruined the grounds of Moselle. Whether equipped with a night vision scope or not, even the most skilled huntsmen could not stop the trial's 72nd witness from taking the stand. When Richard Alexander Murdaugh ambled past the jury box, there was a pervasive sense absolute destruction was imminent as he ventured one final scheme—duping his jury.

By the time it was his turn to testify—or rather test-a-lie—we had heard from a myriad of folks who told of Alex's tenuous relationship with honesty. Case in point, Paul's bombshell testimony, *a la* "the kennel video" had become a penetrating earworm, as the prosecution reviewed this audio again-and-again with witness-after-witness confirming it was Alex's voice. After all, that single piece of evidence quickly transformed Alex's iron-clad alibi into a rust-covered "lalibi." Nonetheless, we were ready and tuned-in with open-ears and an open-mind.

After the defendant confirmed his intention to testify, he was sworn in, then proceeded to ascend the witness stand. Taking his seat, he reached for the gooseneck microphone pushing it closer. When stating his name, he first used the abbreviated form of his middle name, skipping his first entirely; in addition, he used the bygone English pronunciation "Alec." This indicated an air of confidence in his ability to hoodwink his jury while showing us he was unhumbled by the sixteen months he'd already spent jailed. I knew we were in for a show from the moment Alex angled his chair to the right, ever so slightly vaulting it forward, to draw that much closer to us. He settled in for comfort, wiggling side-to-side. It was evident Alex had plans to overstay his welcome. Regarding our reaction to his testimony, Gigi McKelvey stated, "The jury was very intrigued and watched him closely. He maintained eye contact with them, and they with him; only a small few chose to engage in passing glimpses." It was extremely uncomfortable to watch his deep-set dark—unusually dark—eyes meet our individual and collective gazes. For when he did this, it was easy to see the many sides of Alex Murdaugh that fooled so many people. Dick and Jim should have been more honed into their client's non-verbal cues because the white flag of surrender needed to be hoisted long before he took one final wriggle sideways and grabbed the microphone to address *us* with "Good Morning."

Jim Griffin would be the one faced with the herculean task of trying to rehabilitate his pathological liar of a client on the witness stand in real time. Carl Grant applauded Griffin's attempt saying, "he was trying to make chicken salad out of chicken feathers." Jim began the direct examination by sternly, loudly, and pointedly asking Alex if he murdered Paul and Maggie, Jim moved into questioning him first about being at the kennels. Then he followed with inquiries about his motherlode of additional untruths, to which Alex put the blame on anything and anyone but himself. Alex's reply of "Oh what a tangled web we weave" when asked about his habitually forked tongue was pathetic. The only thing I could think of was, after all this time you've had to come up with something—anything—that is all you've got.

Richard Alexander Murdaugh will go down in the annals of history as one of the worst defendants ever to take the witness stand. Details on the origin of this terrible decision are conflicting, which to any reasonable person would be shocking. However, to those who have closely watched Dick and Jim attempt to negotiate the misadventures of Alex Murdaugh, know this is just another ordinary day in bizzarro world. *Forbes* and *The Daily Mail* claim Alex waived his Fifth Amendment rights "against the advice of his counsel," while *Fox Carolina* and *CNN* shifted responsibility, respectively saying, "Alex Murdaugh's attorneys are considering putting him on the stand" and "Alex always wanted to testify." Lastly in their first post-verdict presser, Harpootlian said, "He had no choice but to testify in his murder trial because he had been made out to be a monster who stole from children, crippled people and others." While I remain unclear if Dick was suggesting the prosecution and media colluded or if he was attempting to blame one or the other. The reality is it does not matter who was responsible for the trainwreck because like John Meadors said, "Alex was the most powerful witness against Alex."

Honestly, I was a bit taken aback when I learned he had chosen to waive his Fifth Amendment right and would be taking the stand. My response seemed to be consistent among my fellow jurors and social media users who had such commentary as:

Gigi McKelvey (*Pretty Lies and Alibis* host): With her signature ear-to-ear smile and endearing giggle she told her listeners, It was funny to watch the jury's reaction. They all shifted in their seats. It was obvious they wanted to talk to the person next to them and say, 'Oh my gosh; he's taking the stand.' But they kept their composure and were very attentive during his testimony.

Law & Lumber: Well, there you have it … Alex Murdaugh will testify. Buckle your seatbelts.

Pamela Houston: Well, there goes the rest of my day!

Ollie: Didn't see that coming! I have stuff to do and now can't leave the house.

Britt: His lawyers look terrified

The Curmudgeon: Morning productivity blown

Sardonisms: Me: I don't think the state met its burden. AM: hang on, lemme help

Kay Prine: I've got to get me one of my nervous pills. It may take 2.

EggplantAstronaut: No comment, but they posted a gif that reads "OH MY GOSH! OKAY, IT'S HAPPENING!" The image is from *The Office*, and the characters, with concerned looks, are racing to safety from their cubicles because smoke is pouring from an adjoining room.

As always, Gigi's jury watching skills were on fleek. Likewise, I can vouch for each of these clever quips from the people of X (formerly Twitter) because I would have felt the same way following the trial through cyber space. The rational side of me understood it was truly his only option. The entire world, except for those who live under the proverbial rock, listened to him repeatedly say he was not at the kennels with Maggie and Paul on the night of the murders. However, we would soon hear his voice in the background of a recording that was time-stamped minutes before Paul and Maggie's brutal murders. He attempted to explain away his many reasons for misleading law enforcement for so long, claiming it was his only choice. Former Los Angeles prosecutor, Loni Coombs remarked, "This kennel video is the most important piece of evidence in this case because it explodes the big lie of his alibi."[9] Gigi McKelvey, shared Coombs's sentiment, telling her listeners, "He had to testify. If his lies had gone unanswered, the prosecution would have eaten that for breakfast on closing."

From the moment Alex stood up to place his hand on the "Good Book," an unfamiliar weighted darkness seemed to creep into the courtroom. The storm had gathered and now with its mounting pressure would loom over the jury box waiting to unleash its fury. Throughout the previous five weeks, we'd heard voluminous evidence that painted Alex Murdaugh in the spirit of a ruthless comic book supervillain with dueling personalities—a magnanimous community member/a parasitic thief; a family man/a family annihilator; approachable and convivial legacy lawyer/moody and anxious opioid addict—who no one, not even those closest to him, ever completely knew. Was I, in some way, worried about his unpredictability? Did I think the cross might get too heated and Alex would try to leapfrog the witness stand to pummel Creighton Waters? Certainly, I was not fearful of defying the court's order and considering the financial crimes for something other than motive? I know that a person can be a despicable human and thief, but that bad act does not mean he is a cold-blooded killer.

We were chosen to give him a fair trial, and that is exactly what we did. During deliberations we would give all testimony equal weight. Deciding the guilt or innocence of Alex Murdaugh was in our hands, and we, the jury, were not going to presuppose *anything*. For better or worse, the man was on trial for his life, and he chose to tell us—the jury—his side of the story.

The initial open-mindedness I—Juror 864—held about Alex's choice to testify was non-existent when average, everyday citizen Amie Williams rewatched his testimony. There I sat, again, for hours and *hours* watching this snake oil salesman's infomercial. The second he grabbed that chair and angled it toward where we would have been sitting reaffirmed, we got it right. It was like watching a movie for the second time and noticing things that were otherwise missed, and this time I was angry. I was infuriated by his flagrant disrespect for Creighton Waters; his simple country lawyer schtick; his crocodile tears with runaway snot, and so much more.

Alex's testimony in the courtroom did not noticeably raise my blood pressure, but being fully informed while watching the re-run made my heart pound and face flush. The curious way he would repeat a question like Creighton suddenly began speaking Klingon was an obvious powerplay. Greg Adeline of *WIS News 10* commented, "He would repeat most of the questions he was asked back to the prosecutor. This seemed very deliberative. He was answering it much like a lawyer, often parsing words and being very careful and crafted with his answers." Trial Lawyer Carl B. Grant likens this to Alex's oppositional personality and inflated sense of self- worth saying:

Let's not forget a witness's demeanor is evidence at trial. In the case of Alex, he's not just the defendant but also a witness. It seemed to me his demeanor was this, I'm going to show you, Creighton Waters, that I'm the better trial lawyer. I'm going to match wits with you. I'm going to show you that I'm smarter than you are; I'm more persuasive and have an answer for any question that you throw my way. Bring it on! I'm ready.

In addition to that maneuver, another tactic Alex used frequently was acting just plain ignorant. Such as when Waters mentioned the scheme to defraud the then under-aged sisters, Alaina and Hannah Plyler, "You were doing some fast-talking to teenagers, is that correct?" His response, "I don't know how fast I was talking." I'll admit it; I laughed both times I heard that one. Was this a ruse to try and make us believe he was so distraught about the deaths of Maggie and Paul that he was a mere shell of a man? Maybe we were to think the opioids killed his brain cells?

Listening to Alex's convoluted explanation for telling "the big lie" became tedious. Yes, he had some twists and turns to keep his audience engaged; however, his story was not only bizarre, it was also an insult to both our intelligence and law enforcement. On the stand he claimed it was paranoia that stemmed from his opioid addiction which ultimately led to a distrust in SLED. He also made sure to mention his "growing suspicions as police swabbed his hands for gunpowder residue and asked about his relationship with his family, as well as warnings from his law firm partners about always having a lawyer present when speaking to the police." There are so many things wrong with this, before anyone asked questions or did testing, he lied about his whereabouts to 911 operators. He also said *repeatedly* during his first and second interview with David Owen, the leading agent from SLED, "I understand; you do what you need to do." However, while test-a- lying, he took a brief jaunt into a made for daytime television moment of mistaken identity. In which he asserted he mistook Owen for an investigator that he and his father believed had falsified evidence in a case against long-time family friend, and alleged "fixer" Yemassee police chief Greg Alexander. It was a well-known fact, reinforced through testimony, that the Murdaughs had an unusually cozy relationship with local law-enforcement. So much so, he purportedly "put blue lights in his car with their blessing and carried a badge in case he needed a favor." Although the former would be debunked when TC Smalls (former sheriff of Hampton County) testified this was the first he'd heard of the conversation, and it did not happen.

An article on *Crime and Justice News* beautifully summed up the struggle to buy what he was selling during the two days he talked and talked some more, "To trust his new story, jurors must wrestle with Murdaugh's litany of admitted lies. They will have to decide if they believe this man, who once carried a badge, harbored such misgivings about the officers questioning him that he was willing to mislead them as they hunted for the person who killed his wife and son."

In addition to this outrageousness, we saw him struggle to keep up with the timeline—a fruitless endeavor. We watched Alex's manipulative wheels turn. as he tried to plug the more noticeable holes in his new narrative, but he just could not do it. As Creighton Waters mentioned during cross-examination, Alex was manufacturing a revised alibi in real time right before his jury's eyes, in which he could recall trifles about the night of June 7, 2021 like his phone falling between the seat when leaving Almeda. But he could not remember the last words spoken between him and Maggie. *Substack* writer Anne Fernandez masterly offers a summation of the longest fourteen hours of my life when saying:

> Murdaugh squirmed hardest when asked to acknowledge his obvious advantages. Born into a prominent—he did not like this word—family of lawyers and prosecutors who had a close relationship with law enforcement from whom he benefited because of their intergenerational wealth and power. He appeared indefatigable in his hedging and hawing, redirecting and redefining — the man filibustered so long that the jury might have forgotten why they were

there. Survivors of manipulation by liars, cheaters, abusers, or thieves were rightly warned that watching it could be a difficult emotional experience.

When I came across this post all I could think was, "Girl, get out of my head!" More specifically, the way Fernandez mentions him squirming when having to admit that he was successful and wealthy. I'd like to say, he had me squirming, but mine was caused from anger. I wanted to pop up and say, "Sir, we've seen that house, your beach house, expensive toys, and a Gucci receipt; the fourteen of us will likely *never* have a tiny sliver of the luxury you once enjoyed." Secondly, as a survivor, I could not agree more. The traits of an abuser seldom change—it's just coming from a different person. They are called warning signs and red flags to make these wretched, feral (sub)humans easily detectable.

Secondly, it did not go unnoticed by any of us that Alex enjoyed the benefit of sitting at trial for five weeks, enabling him to cherry-pick from the testimony he deemed beneficial. For example, Alex tried to cross through mistakes he'd made because of data presented during testimony in his repetition of phrases like, "I know I was off in my timing because of the records" and "with the benefit of the data, I now recall." Similarly, it was especially repellent to hear him steal testimony from brokenhearted family and friends to boost his image. For instance, Marian Proctor was the witness who said, "Maggie was a girl's girl but embraced having boys and going hunting and fishing." John Marvin and Rogan Gibson are the two who regaled Paul as "fiercely loyal."

Alex should have continued to plagiarize from these same sources because when he went rogue, it was maddening. In the hours of recordings, we watched and rewatched, he never referred to the Maggie as "Mags" or called Paul "Paw Paw." Only Alex Murdaugh could turn something endearing like a nickname into melodramatic theatre. There is no way Dick and Jim suggested he use it repeatedly. I'll give the man some grace and say, after the fifth time it got irritating and began to feel disingenuous. Per usual, social media had definite thoughts about Nicknamegate. Some of the most clever, from unnamed users include: 1) "Alex Murdaugh seems to think that repeating Paw-Paw nonstop is his best defense 2) "He's gonna make #PawPaw trend for a week" and 3) "It's official folks, add Paw-Paw and Mags to your Murdaugh Family Nicknames Bingo Card 4) "If I never hear Pawpaw again in my entire life, it will be too soon." Call me partial, I must say "Sanndeemm" won the hearts of fourteen Colleton County residents when he said, "Pretty sure, by this time, the jurors have completely forgotten the initial start of testimony when AM dramatically said he did not kill Mags and Pawpaw."

Our guilty verdict rested first on the presented evidence which illustrated Alex had the motive, means, and opportunity. And the defendant's testimony served to fill any aperture of doubt that may have been in my head and heart. Carl Grant said, this case came down to "the why vs. the lie," and the result was a test of believability. There was not one witness who could attest to Alex having a modicum of honesty. Dick and Jim's client, and dear friend, may have fooled some trial watchers into believing he was credible and affable. However, he still lost in the courtroom and in the court of public opinion, which included some fascinating insight from renowned body language analysts, proving we got it right.

Janine Driver, in a *CNN* interview, began by discussing his speech patterns. The news anchor, in an exasperated and exhausted tone, mirrored exactly how we, the jury, felt about how much Alex talked and mostly about nothing. Driver noted the words we say can reveal just as much as our movements when analyzing deception. She drew attention to statement analysis which are words that have hidden meanings. The strongest denial is always a "No," but to overexplain or question and accuse is overselling, which he is doing when using words like unequivocally or a phrase like "absolutely not." In doing this, he is reminding us that "truthful people convey; liars, try to convince." Piggy backing off Driver's analysis on speech, body language analyst, Lillian Glass, commented on Alex being hyperarticulate by imparting extensive specificity, such as he did with trying to turn Paul over using his belt loop. Further saying, providing too much detail is a big indicator of deception. Some notable and curious mannerisms Alex displayed on the stand include, but are not limited to:

> **Dr. G**: During cross-examination his posture changed to look like he was trying to hide or appear smaller. When Creighton is trying to get Alex to acknowledge his privilege, he begins shifting in his chair, indicating a level of discomfort—almost like he wanted to get up and leave. When asked if he was a family annihilator, he grew quite angry. He took deep breaths showing his heart is pumping harder

because when we feel anxious or stressed, this is our physiological response. When discussing checking Paul, we see an outward display of intense emotion, and the emotion gets shut off completely when he has to explain something in an intellectual way; it's all or nothing, and that is chilling.

Janine Driver (Court TV): He shook his head, yes but was saying no. This is relevant because we are responding to the second, alternate dialogue coming into our head, which tells me there is more to the story. But his inner eyebrows pulled together and up which is indicative of true authentic sadness, for what is unknown. Is this grief or selfish sadness? He also does a lot of tongue protrusion. This happens when we are deep in concentration and is seen a lot with deception and embarrassment; we often stick our tongue out when we are lying, so this was suspicious to me. We saw that he had dry mouth on the stand because lying causes the membranes in our mouth to become dry, as the blood flow is changing.

I know avid trial watchers, especially those riveted by *SC vs. Richard Alexander Murdaugh*, did not need a body language analyst to validate he is a lying liar who lies. However, it is captivating to learn that Alex got away with so much deceit, his body was betraying him the entire time.

Both legal and body language experts agree that Alex was attempting to put on an Oscar winning performance for us. A friend of mine happened to attend the trial on Alex's first day of testimony. Months after the verdict was rendered, she shared a story with me that truly shows his powerful—but not powerful enough—acting skills. Courties, a moniker for Court TV devotees, know when they see the State Seal, court is not in session. The action may stop for viewers in TV land, but not for those in the courtroom. It is here the trial watcher can see, and even hear, the unexpected. These moments are raw and give a unique glimpse into the participants. The rantings of indignant, pompous attorneys who had heard "overruled" one too many times is quite comical. The kindness of reporters, such as Valerie Bauerlein from the *Wall Street Journal*, and podcasters, like *Cup of Justice's* Eric Bland, who pause for a picture while racing to the snack machine is wildly heartwarming. However, witnessing a defendant's actions when the jury is not present, and the cameras *are not* rolling can be repellant. Before the afternoon session commenced, a handcuffed Alex Murdaugh, flanked by bailiffs, returned first to the courtroom. Of course, trial watchers in the gallery were both affixed and appalled by his demeanor. Murdaugh was smiling, laughing, and joking with the guards. This man, after all, was testifying in his own double murder trial and fighting for his life. When Judge Newman stated, "Bring the Jury," Alex must have heard the slamming of a clapboard and a shout of "Take Two." In no time, he resumed the "Poor Pitiful Me" show, picking up exactly where he left off. Without missing a beat, he started bawling, wiping runaway snot, and professing his innocence. Alex undoubtedly felt he deserved the "best leading man," and Team Murdaugh wasted no time in publicly applauding his performance. We were all in agreement that taking the stand was not only necessary but also a horrible idea. Creighton Waters knew—he knew hands down—Alex would testify and lie to our face. If you give a narcissist a microphone, their ego will prove too powerful, especially since Alex knew   the world was watching him. The more he yammered in an attempt to match the shiny new facts learned at trial to the meandering and inconsistent fabrications he told law enforcement, the worse he got. Quite pointedly, he was so ready for a battle of wits with Creighton that even a fistful of hush your mouth pills could not have stopped that train wreck. Alex Murdaugh personified Lawrence O'Donnell's sentiment, "Practically, every defense lawyer knows that the jury desperately wants to hear from the defendant and that the only reason not to put him on the stand is that he is soooo (sic) guilty that every answer he gives after his name will eradicate any shred of reasonable doubt."

CHAPTER 9:
HERE COMES THE JUDGE

When asked about the role of a judge, Chief Justice Roberts replied, "Judges are like umpires. Umpires don't make the rules; they apply them. The role of an umpire and a judge is critical; they make sure everybody plays by the rules. Nobody ever went to a ball game to see the umpire." Had I not spent six weeks in Judge Clifton Newman's courtroom, I would be in whole-hearted agreement with Roberts. People had various reasons for attending the trial of Alex Murdaugh, and I am willing to bet each person who sat in the gallery of the Colleton County Courthouse was eager to watch Judge Newman in action. Looking back at my time served, I imagine Lady Justice gave us a little wink from behind her blindfold, knowing we would be fulfilling our civic duty under a judicial legend.

Many people are drawn to their chosen career because of a significant experience from their youth. Judge Newman was no different. For him, his interest piqued when cast in a high school play based on a 1950s desegregation case. He played a New York City lawyer who "came to save the people." Elaborating further on this consequential role, Newman proclaimed, "Coming from a small rural farming community it helped me create a vision of something greater than I otherwise would have had exposure to at home." In a commencement address Newman gave earlier this year at Coastal Carolina University (May 2024), he shared a similar nugget of wisdom with the graduating class telling them, "take it from a country boy from Greeleyville, South Carolina, who spent 24 years on the bench. It's not where you start; it is where, and how, you finish." In a society plagued by a false sense of self-importance and entitlement, it's rare to see people recognize and appreciate a meager beginning. Judge Newman is among the cherished few who embraces and celebrates a humble start. Never once feeling ashamed of his heritage, or taking it for granted, he *still* recognizes the pivotal role it has played in every stage of his career. As for where Judge Newman sees himself in the annals of the South Carolina judiciary, he applauded the burgeoning diversity among the legal landscape, maintaining, "I have seen a great number of talented people become lawyers who would not have had the chance before. When I became a lawyer, there were very few African American attorneys, as well as very few women." Remembering his early days as a prosecutor, he considers the pursual of a judgeship to be a natural career progression; noting how he consistently turned to the judge in pursuit of attaining some sort of relief for his client. He thought, one day, it would be nice to give back by issuing such orders, calling the role of a jurist an "… awesome and challenging responsibility. We carry the weight of the judicial system on our shoulders, seeking to always dispense an appropriate and accurate measure of fairness." This devotion to Lady Justice was evident from the very first moment of jury selection straight through to the final tap of his gavel.

Presiding over the Lowcountry's trial of the century did not happen at random. Judge Newman's name was not picked out of a hat nor chosen by a lottery system. He was appointed at will by S.C. Supreme Court Chief (Ret.) Justice Donald Beatty. Newman was hand-picked, in part, for his "level-headed approach, cool judgement, and commitment to justice." As well as for his previous successes in presiding over high-profile cases, such as *SC vs. Michael Slager* (the cop who fatally shot Walter Scott) and *SC vs. Nathanial Rowland* (the fake Uber driver who savagely murdered Samantha Josephson). As reflected below, praise for The Honorable Judge Clifton Newman resonated far and wide from pressrooms, courthouses to the marble and granite hallways of South Carolina's capital building:

Jennifer Hawes (*Post and Courier*): Although the judge said virtually nothing as the attorneys sparred for 40 minutes, he was easily the most powerful person in the courtroom.

Kevin Fisher (*Post and Courier*): It's hard to imagine a steadier hand or calmer presence than Judge Newman. He is cerebral but decisive, a judge who makes quick and clear rulings, handling it all with a quiet but powerful dignity that engendered confidence in the court.

Jared Newman (Port Royal Defense Attorney): I couldn't think of a better judge they could put on this pile of awful that's going on.

Bakari Sellers (Columbia Attorney): Judge Newman is a jurist beyond reproach.

Thomas McElveen (SC State Senator): Judge Newman is the very best we have to offer here. He is a pillar of our judiciary and our bar.

Roger Kirby (SC Representative): Judge Newman is a steady judicial hand, exuding wisdom and unfailing integrity, a testament to the highest aspirations for the judiciary in South Carolina.

John Meadors (Columbia Attorney): He was the shining star of the trial. South Carolina was well represented, by his graceful, iron hand.

Of the hundreds of comments, I reviewed across a variety of social media sites, every post that mentioned Judge Newman was complimentary. There was not a single outrageous post from attention seeking agitators. No one utilized internet platforms as a bully pulpit. Being contrary for the sake of a reaction was *so* twenty twenty-two, waning in favor after *Depp* v. *Heard*; although, at present (2024), Karen Read looks to be bringing contrary back with brute force. In the wake of the sentencing, Murdaugh's paltry enclave of conspiracy theorists even went on a months' long hiatus. That is until their warped imaginations were reignited by the truckload of manufactured fodder Dick and Jim dumped in front of the South Carolina Court of Appeals last Fall (September 2023), but more about that later.

Judge Newman's decades of wisdom were apparent each time he took the bench, as was his abiding concern for our protection and overall comfort, both in and out of the courtroom. We *felt* the kindness trial watchers only got to see on television. For example, since we had court on Valentine's Day, he surprised us with goodie bags of candy to thank us for our service. That was such a thoughtful gesture. It is my hope he knows how much we appreciated it. It turned out, chocolate was the perfect comfort food for what ended up being a very difficult day of testimony. Who would not need a Snickers bar or three after Marion Proctor's heartbreaking testimony and Dick's hostile assault on Dr. Riemer's credibility. Although his crusade would prove futile, it was difficult to hear and made several of us feel exceedingly uncomfortable.

One of the many things I admire about Judge Newman is the way he showed firm authority but remained diplomatic. I once considered myself a patient person, until sitting in his courtroom. I do not know how he did it. Almost daily the same few people—who shall remain nameless—lingered dangerously close to the line that separates decorum from incivility. While others, with hubris ablaze, drove a Mack Truck of flagrant disregard straight through the blockade. It was truly remarkable how, with the patience of Job, Judge Newman never wavered in showing the offending parties grace and respect.

Putting the defendant's legacy aside, and just taking the trial itself into consideration, *a lot* of peculiar things happened during those six weeks. Some are mundane, or silly, while others perpetuate Southern stereotypes. Beginning with the large cast of characters which took me a few days to categorize who went where, especially since we were unable to take notes in real time:

Family: John Marvin, Randy, Buster
Law Partners: Danny Henderson, Ronnie Crosby, Mark Ball.
Paul's Friends: Rogan, Nolan, Wills.

For me, repetition was central in keeping each person in their proper place, making it easier to recall who knew what and when they knew it. The family had a penchant for nicknaming everyone *and* everything. This provided an added layer of confusion in the initial game of who's who; however, for the Murdaughs, it would be more accurate to say, a game of is that a who, or is it a what:

Homes: Moselle, Almeda, Edisto.
People: Big Red (Alex), Handsome (Alex's Father), Bo (any male friend).
Cars: Dolly (newer F-250) White Boy (White F-150), Buster's Truck (older Black F-150).
Shot Gun: Bo Whoop

I'm quite certain our friends to the North, East, West, and across the pond enjoyed the colloquialisms and may have felt slightly vindicated for stereotyping southerners based on shows like *Welcome to Myrtle Manor* and *Duck Dynasty*. It will be a minute before anyone forgets Alex's complimentary master class on how to extract a chicken from the mouth of a dog. Should I ever have to rescue poultry from the canine jowls of death, the defendant's post-removal wisdom to "put the chicken aside and let it do what a chicken does" will echo in my mind. I don't mention these things to mock, but to say it was moments like these which provided some much-needed levity. It's difficult to imagine any such flash of provincial flair happening in the courtrooms of Judge Wapner or Judge Judy.

Due to the duration of *SC vs Richard Alexander Murdaugh*, they wanted to ensure there would be a sizable pool of alternates. We still numbered eighteen until Day 16 (of what would be a 28-day trial) when Covid infiltrated the courthouse, picking off both staff and 2 jurors. Through this Judge Newman remained resolute, refusing to bend to Dick's squawking about preempting the proceedings. Instead, he implemented mandatory testing for all jurors and remaining alternates, along with optional masking.

In a previous chapter, I spoke extensively about the bomb threat, yet due to the potential it had to derail the trial indefinitely, it bears some brief repetition. After learning the courthouse received a call about a bomb in the judge's chamber, he announced, in measured tone, everyone needed to leave the building. Among the evacuees was his spouse of over fifty years who attended the trial every day. I am fairly poised in stressful situations; however, I believe the threat of deadly explosives might be my tipping point.

If an infectious disease and an inmate with an appetite for making felonious prank calls, never roweled Judge Newman, would anything? Would the shenanigans of Alex's defense counsel—one with itchy twitter fingers and the other channeling the Godfather—vex the robed southern gentleman? Would the Murdaugh family's irreverence for courtroom protocol rile the softspoken jurist? Would a rogue juror with the gift of gab inflame America's beloved judge? The answer to these questions is a resounding, NO.

Evidently, mere days away from closing arguments, Jim Griffin decided to advocate for his client by taking to social media. Upon returning from a three-day weekend, the wait for court to begin was a bit longer than usual. Since mornings always started with both sides sorting housekeeping details, we speculated there was more to review due to the Presidents' Day holiday. Unbeknownst to us at the time, this was not an ordinary late start. The twenty-first day of *SC* vs. *Richard Alexander Murdaugh* would be brought to trial watchers by the letter "X." Over the three-day weekend, Jim "reposted" an op-ed from *The Washington Post* entitled, "Alex Murdaugh Trial Reveals a Sloppy Investigation." Months later, when I would learn of this ridiculousness, wide-eyed and slack jawed, I yelped, "WHAT in the world?" Griffin was no newb to trying a case during the digital age, but he may need some help with the intricacies of the platform. When Judge Newman addressed his hijinks, before a packed courtroom, Jim very matter-of-factly replied, "it has been taken down." and "all I did was 'retweet.'" As recently as July (2024), while researching something else entirely, I discovered the op-ed remained on his profile page with its original date of posting (2/18/23). That does not sound like Jim removed the article, as he reported to Judge Newman. Secondly, the two squared arrows icon that indicates a "retweet" were nowhere in sight. This feels calculated, and Jim Griffin should be grateful that Judge Newman trusted his assertions. With no follow-up from him or court staff, the only consequence of his recklessness was the bench's mild-mannered admonishment:

> I have received emails concerning a social media post by Mr. Griffin. It commented on witnesses' testimony and the quality of the investigation by the state. There is nothing in South Carolina's ethical rules for attorneys that specifically states lawyers are prohibited from criticizing witnesses during trial or mentioning their current case. I think it goes against the spirit of the law. It does not pass the feel test. Moving forward, you should not post or repost anything that would give me or the general public pause. The jurors were instructed not to discuss the case and obviously that did not extend to the lawyers, but it is not good practice.

I believe any avid trial watcher could, within seconds, cite a judge who would have never been that diplomatic. Judge Mary Marlowe Sommer, the jurist who presided over the trial of *Rust* armorer, Hannah Gutierrez-Reed, comes first to my mind. At sentencing, Sommer gave Hannah a scathing tongue lashing and told her exactly what she thought about her jailhouse phone calls—just moments before giving Gutierrez-Reed the maximum sentence of eighteen months for involuntary manslaughter. On that day, the often-tacit Judge Sommer, spoke loudly and carried a life-sized gavel. Inmates are reminded at the beginning of each conversation that it will be recorded. Do they think the little voice over on the other end is just clowning around? The things Hannah said to her friends and family about the lead prosecutor, the jury, and even the jurist were appalling. To say she sounded entitled and spoiled during these caustic rants is putting it mildly.

If social media were a person, Dick and Jim would be their abusive partner. They will exploit her popularity when it serves to push a given agenda. Dick and Jim have both used her reach to drive their "Alex was wronged" narrative. When they aren't kneeling at the foot of Alex's prisoned issued shower slides, Dick may court her to ferret out campaign contributions, and Jim may woo her to promote his new podcast. However, if she dares to speak the truth or goes in search of facts, they will publicly shame and devalue her. For example, when his plan to push the "botched investigation" was foiled by Judge Newman, it was all social media's fault. Jim Griffin, speaking on behalf of #TeamMurdaugh, can be seen giving her the Heisman in the CW's docuseries *Crime*

Nation. Casting blame on the court of public opinion, he asserted, "On social media people can just unload. It's not a place for news; it's more like a gossip column. It is where hearsay about the Murdaughs caught wind and negatively impacted the family. The disinformation from social media worked its way into the minds of the jurors." My response to this absurdity is twofold. First, I would like to say, Mr. Griffin, I must have misunderstood something. For one, it sounded like you were suggesting we lied during jury selection when asked about our familiarity with the case and how frequently we used social media. Then if that was not enough, you also implied we disregarded our juror's oath and researched the case. Furthermore, you have implied we not only lack our God given ability to think critically but that we are also fools who cannot separate factual insight from speculative yip-yap (your client's word, not mine)—and that is very offensive. Was this some sort of tactic aimed at trying to catch one of us perusing our socials so you and Dick could leverage a mistrial, or testing the waters for a larger more diabolical plan? I will pray Jim (and Dick) find the eventual strength to blame the real killer of Maggie and Paul—the *one* person to whom all the evidence points—Richard Alexander Murdaugh.

The next installment of Dick and Jim's kangaroo court offers an astonishing look at an OG "good ole boy" with more moxie than Alex had opioids. Emblazoned in the memory of every juror and trial watcher is the iconic image of Dick Harpootlian—South Carolina's lawyer mob boss wannabe aiming a firearm in open court. Who can forget how they felt when the grey-haired, septuagenarian, with an ear-to-ear smirk wryly said, "I don't know how to do this without pointing it at anybody." Adding to our collective discomfort was Dick's inability to maintain his grip under the heft of the .300 Blackout Rifle. Clad in a dark suit accented with extra fine pinstripes or wrinkles (my memory and the online photo are both unclear), he fumbled and made a slight pivot left, leaving the entire prosecution team staring down the barrel of an assault rifle. This prompted the aspiring mafioso to sneer, "it's tempting." The entire incident was insensitive, tone deaf, and lest we forget, unlawful. This weapon was admitted into evidence because it was nearly identical to the one which killed Maggie. For me personally, this little stunt took my breath away. I was horrified; the only thing I could say was, "No; No; this is not happening." My reaction would have been the same had Creighton Waters (or any of his team members) acted in such an irresponsible and dangerous manner. Another juror found this so disconcerting, they even brought up how uncomfortable it made them feel during an interview with SLED officials regarding the false allegations I will discuss in a later chapter.

Alex's family members, some more than others, carried themselves in a manner that suggested they felt immune from courtroom rules. Ironically, the worst was the in-custody accused murderer who was simultaneously stockpiling indictments for financial crimes. In October (2021) Alex quickly learned he depleted his cache of get out of jail free cards. He could not seem to reckon that the decades of invincibility he once enjoyed were forever in the rearview. Living as an SCDC inmate for fifteen months prior to the double murder trial did nothing to convince him his days as a VIP were over. Likely feeling he had nothing to lose, Alex often hovered over the threshold separating conformity from defiance. Have you ever seen a defendant with a stash of hard candy? I had never witnessed any such thing until *SC* vs. *Richard Alexander Murdaugh*. Dick and Jim were steady passing him hard candy, just like a parent trying to keep their child quiet during Sunday service. File what I am about to state under gossip or rumor, if you wish. I was told Alex preferred anything peppermint. The strong flavoring in peppermint stimulates the mucous membranes and salivary glands and is a known irritant that causes watery eyes. The innuendo of this fact is yours to decide.

When Court TV cameras cut away, pool photographers and reporters were there making sure trial watchers did not miss any key moments. During court recesses the media had a lot to say about the defendant's improper contact with family members. One of the most talked about photos is of Alex patting Buster on the backside as he passes him, on the way to his holding cell. This" tushy tap" was seen globally and went viral almost instantly. Journalist Liz Farrell, with her keen insight and astute wit, referred to this image as "a picture of absurdity, of privilege, of power, of forgiveness, of loyalty, of longing, of abuse, of bullying, of coercion, a family, of control, of entitlement, of sadness, of broken hearts, and of love." Some may think these instances of Alex pushing the constraints of protocol are "no big deal." This is unequivocally false, for once again, the world has very telling evidence of the Murdaughs' blatant disregard for the rule of law, both in and out of the courtroom.

Each new media account of the family's tomfoolery reignited public outrage. Alex was spotted fist bumping and talking with family members. The Murdaugh tribe—including the defendant—were reported to have been seen passing notes between one another. The defense counsel bent the rules too, causing Alex to get "arrested on a misdemeanor warrant issued by Colleton County." This happened when Dick and Jim told Lynne (his sister) that Alex requested a book which she could just give to them, when it first needed to go through the proper channels for examination. Each of the parties involved in BookGate 2023 *knows* the rules, including his sister—a career victims advocate for the courts in Summerville, South Carolina.

I am in *NO* way being Pro-Alex when I question why he was the only one who faced any repercussions, but I am calling out a system that failed to hold the others accountable in some capacity. For an FYI because I know you're just as curious as I was, the book was nothing scandalous like OJ Simpson's *If I Did It*. The novel that gave the Internet something to talk about for a weekend was John Grisham's *The Judge's List*.

Legal analyst Emily D. Baker told her podcast audience, many times over, the preferential treatment shown to Alex, his family, and his legal team is unheard of. The former prosecutor was gobsmacked; explaining that in her 16+ years' experience, she has *never* (*never*, *never*, *never*) seen an "in-custody defendant who is on trial for a double homicide allowed the freedom to touch anyone. EVER!" Noting that in Los Angeles, if a defendant tries to touch anyone in the gallery, they are going to get tazed if not tazed then tackled. This is what Alex Murdaugh, being treated differently by the system, looks like.

There were further reports of Murdaugh mischief that I failed to notice from the jury box, either because I was engrossed in testimony, or my view was obstructed by a wandering Dick Harpootlian. Alex's sister, Lynne, was not the only Murdaugh misfit. Buster made his own headlines numerous times during those six weeks. While he was on the receiving "end" of Alex's uninvited posterior love pat, his own actions created a flurry of social media chatter. For example, when Mark Tinsley, attorney for the Beach family, was approaching the stand, Buster can be seen biting the cuticle of his "bad boy" finger. His acrimony toward Tinsley is striking. Pundits could not seem to agree if he was, indeed, chewing on his cuticle out of nervousness or if he was making an inappropriate gesture. *The Independent* stated the Murdaugh cadre had been "issued several warnings for their errant behavior, eventually being moved to the back of the courtroom and were only one wrong move away from being dismissed entirely." Buster's fiery red hair appears to match an equally fiery temper. The publication also indicated they were asked to move several rows back to put significant space between them and the defendant. After the directive was given, Buster allegedly kicked over a water bottle in anger. Lynne— like Buster— became quite incensed with court officials when she was called out for her misconduct.

In an earlier chapter, I said John Meadors's rebuttal was magical—aside from being an example of spoken genius—it muzzled the trolls for a while. This will come as a surprise to *no one*, Judge Newman was able to replicate the same level of silence. These two men achieved the impossible—they made cyber kindness cool. Of the 150+ comments I sifted through, each held him in such high esteem:

From users of X:

@theshamingofjay: I feel like the reason we all love Judge Newman so much is that in a world of hucksters and frauds at every corner, it is so rare to see someone every day with such brilliance, integrity, kindness, calmness and patience. The Honorable Judge Newman. Thank you.

@petestrom: Does anyone disagree that he sets the gold standard for how a judge conducts a trial?

@RutRoJamz: if nothing else, I hope he will be a guiding light and a mentor to those coming behind him. He was the calm in the storm, and the way he handled his courtroom was beyond admirable.

@lorihellis: So impressed with Judge Newman. I've appeared in front of a lot of judges, and he is amazing.

@N2IT8: just an amazing wise and impressive gentleman. A bright spot in this sordid Murdaugh mess.

From Users of YouTube:

@mosessupposes2571: Judge Newman has the kind of backbone and integrity that we wish everyone in the legal system had.

@user-bc2jy7cp9g: "Get him out," said this fantastic Judge.

@aprilb835: Judge Newman is my hero. A calm, thoughtful presence of a man who delivers his message with humility and respect for those who never earned such treatment from another human. What a wonderful authority to have behind the gavel.

Once the trial ended, it was nice to settle back into my daily scrolls through social media. It was exceptionally heartwarming to see Judge Newman pop up in my feed periodically. No—we are not Facebook friends. However, since gaveling out a temporary release from Murdaugh World, "America's Judge," once again, allowed himself the freedom to do the things he enjoys. Even if an outing to watch his beloved Lady Gamecocks meant impromptu meet-and-greets complete with selfies galore. I presume Judge Newman considered his daily life might look a little different following the murder trial, but I highly doubt "always oblige your adoring fans" was ever on his radar as something to consider.

Judge Newman reached South Carolina's mandatory age for judicial retirement (72) in November of 2023, forcing him to leave the bench. However, it would not take him long to realize he was not quite ready to have a permanent seat on the sidelines. In April (2024) Michael Dewitt of *Greenville News*, reported Judge Newman took a job with JAMS and will be based in the Atlanta Resolution Center. The group was formally known as Judicial Arbitration and Mediation Services. It is recognized as "the largest private provider of alternative dispute resolution (ADR) services worldwide." As we've come to expect from the man, the myth, the legend, he spoke humbly of joining the JAMS team of panelists, remarking, "With over 23 years of experience on the bench, I am committed to resolving ordinary, complex, and high-profile matters at JAMS using the same even-tempered and consistent approach that has served me well throughout my career." It is now my turn to say the words you so often said to us—Thank you for your service. Few, if any can dispute, South Carolina's loss is Georgia's gain.

CHAPTER 10:
THE ROOM
WHERE IT HAPPENS

Upon our return from Moselle, there was a recognized surge of adrenaline rushing through the jury room(s) during our lunch break and showed no sign of stalling when closing arguments began. Likewise, there was something I can only describe as a sense of nervous excitement rippling through the courtroom well and gallery. Save for one, Alex Murdaugh, it was not our lives on the line, so why was the sense of nervousness so pervasive? Trial Watchers recognized there were no winners in this case, and to feel a sense of excitement for a guilty verdict would be celebrating the loss of Buster's only living parent. This extraordinary vibe served as a signal to us, that the end was fast approaching and slowing down for *no one*.

In less than twenty-four hours, Court TV would start their iconic "Verdict Watch" clock. Millions of people across the globe would soon be held prisoner by their screen as each hour, minute, and second, that we deliberated ticked away. The network masterfully describes this as:

The period when the anticipation steadily rises, as everyone gathers outside of the courtroom to wait. Time can hang heavy in those minutes, hours, and sometimes even days. Then it happens, a bailiff walks into the lobby and says the magic words, 'the jury has reached a verdict.' Then time suddenly slams into motion as everyone rushes into the courtroom preparing themselves for the final moment of justice.

Having not been an avid trial watcher prior to doing this lengthy civic duty, I had no idea these audiences experienced such an intense angst, regardless of which side of justice they aired. From what I could discern from my research, there was a sense of optimism that we, the jury, would be able to cast fear aside and embrace the results proven during testimony. Doing so would eradicate the coercion which held Colleton County, and her neighboring communities, in its sinewy clutches for decades.

Once Judge Newman concluded his charge, the case would be turned over to twelve people who were strangers to the defendant. The very twelve people Alex Murdaugh chose as the jury of his peers. This was the moment we had been working toward for six long weeks. We listened to the testimony of every witness; we learned the facts of the case, as well as some interesting alternative facts. His guilt was clear to me. I wondered if my fellow jurors arrived at the same conclusion. If I was the lone wolf and they believed he was not guilty, could they convince me otherwise, or would I be the one to hang the jury? I had so many hypotheticals whirling through my mind.

When Judge Newman announced, he was now going to instruct us on the law as it applied to the indictments against Alex Murdaugh, I swallowed hard knowing this was it. There would be no more witnesses, exhibits, or surly protestations from the defense. The passage below is just a snippet taken from various places within our twenty-one-page jury charge. I chose the lines which I felt most powerfully illustrated the weight of our responsibility and the enormity of the task before us:

Madam forelady, and members of the jury, you have heard the testimony, received the evidence and heard the arguments of the state and the defendant. Under the constitution and laws of South Carolina, you are the finders of the facts in this case. This is a matter solely for you, the jury, to determine. You may believe a small portion of a witness's testimony and disregard the larger or vice versa. All of these things you will consider bearing in mind that you should give the defendant the benefit of any reasonable doubt. Evidence of other crimes or bad acts cannot be used to show that the defendant is a bad person and therefore is more likely to have committed the crime for which he is accused. You may not consider evidence of other crimes and bad acts for any purpose other than as it relates to the motive of the defendant.

This was it. In just minutes we—at long last—would not only be allowed to discuss the case but discuss it with one another. That thought alone was liberating. As I noted earlier, some days were simply heartbreaking. Some days the testimony was difficult, not in the sense that it was hard to understand (aside from the DNA evidence, of course), but difficult in that it laid bare the depths of human depravity. On days like this, I just wanted to talk to someone—anyone—beginning with those who were witnessing the same horrors right alongside of me. As social beings the desire to unburden ourselves is almost instinctual. An empathetic ear would have done wonders to remove, or at least alleviate some of the heft, from the blanket of sorrow that seemed to envelop us more-and-more with each passing day.

This shared experience began among eighteen individuals, which illness and circumstance would eventually winnow down to a baker's dozen on the final day of trial. However, in the end, only twelve would sit around the deliberation table. It was unreal to think from the moment our forewoman signed the first of four indictments, which would indicate our verdict, this body of twelve would share a secret. Even the media who had been perched outside of the courthouse for six weeks and those in TV land who tirelessly covered the trial night-after-night, would remain unaware of *our* breaking news. Confident we delivered justice for Maggie and Paul, it was troubling to think this unanimous verdict would essentially orphan Buster, changing his life forever. For a finite amount of time—we the jury—would know something the rest of the world was breathless to learn.

As Judge Newman was winding down our charge, I was so swept up in how surreal it felt, I nearly missed his departing words, "Now ladies and gentlemen, I will send you to your jury room. Once you have reached a verdict you will knock on the door, advise the bailiff, and we will bring you out to receive the verdict." Showtime was nigh; we would soon be in deliberations to opine the guilt or innocence of the Lowcountry's most notorious criminal. Everyone assembled in the courtroom rose for us to make our penultimate exit from the jury box. With only one back-up juror to spare, we survived six long and arduous weeks that had more twists and turns than an amusement ride at Cedar Point— "The Roller Coaster Capital of the World." Having nearly depleted the alternate pool, most recently as that morning, the defense asked that she (our final alternate) remain on the premises until a verdict was rendered. Creighton Waters and his team concurred with their request. Once through the courtroom doors, the alternate was escorted by a bailiff to another room on the second floor. It was unreal to think that was the first time we would ever enter and exit the jury room as a body of twelve. It was also the first and final time we'd sit around the deliberation table together (well at the Colleton County Courthouse, that is).

The jury room was painted a warm shade of periwinkle blue, and the two shortest walls were each adorned with three windows, cloaking it in a natural light we were unaware was so desperately needed. They also provided proof those days marched forward, per usual. Although if challenged, some of us might double down and insist the Lowcountry was experiencing an inaugural foray into polar nights—the 24 hours of nighttime only otherwise found in the most northern and southern regions of Earth. After all, we left and returned home in the dark. Our eight-hour days were much different than those of counsel, staff, media, and spectators, as they were permitted to amble around inside and outside of the courthouse during their breaks. We, however, were confined to a restricted area for our own protection. A friend even commented once on what an early spring we had in 2023. I replied, "I don't remember that." To which she quipped, "You spent six weeks dressed for cold, windy mornings, knowing you would be outside waiting for the court transportation. Then, when it was time to do the routine, in reverse, the sun had settled in for the evening, while temperatures made haste to fall and revert to something more akin to the season. Those of us who did not need a smoke break never seemed to venture outside. This does not mean we were held prisoner; no one felt the need to ask, I suppose. The bailiffs and other court staff were so accommodating, I am sure they would not have begrudged us the opportunity to take in some fresh air and feel the sun on our skin.

Filling our jury room from the center was a mahogany conference table whose primary function was to serve as an all you can eat buffet which displayed the day's snacks down its center, almost creating a dividing line. It was surrounded by twelve dark brown pleather chairs. Each was thinly cushioned and accented with gold upholstery tacks running up-and-down their sides. Additional seating could be found tightly pressed, arm rest-to-arm rest, against the longest two walls. The cliché "packed in like sardines" was an understatement, at best, especially in the beginning weeks when we numbered eighteen. Although we gelled quickly and became fast friends who genuinely enjoyed one another's company, it did not take us too long to realize the jury rooms in the historic Colleton County Courthouse were designed with a twelve-juror panel, and maybe two alternates, in mind.

Most of us preferred to pass the time talking about something— anything—to help distract us from the case. Others preferred to spend our breaks in a more subdued atmosphere that may be better conducive to reading, meditating, or just surveilling the pandemonium taking place on the streets below. While they could not oblige our need for a larger room by knocking down a wall, they allowed us to use a nearby office (Jury Room *B*) which belonged to a newly retired judge who was still called in from time to time. I bet he was ecstatic his services were not needed amid the chaos that defined *SC* vs *Richard Alexander Murdaugh*.

The windows in Jury Room *A* overlooked a parking lot filled with food trucks that had a constant bustling of tourists, media, and attorneys. Even the owners and employees from nearby businesses who were hungry for a fresh lunch choice, and hopeful they'd spot a celebrity, stopped by the food truck court. Jury Room *B* had the best view to people watch. Its windows overlooked the front lawn, where eager media gathered each day preparing for their upcoming live reports. This was also the spot where ardent, hopeful trial watchers stood in a line, talking to strangers who became friends, hoping the doors of justice did not slam shut in their face before securing the day's admission badge. As a brief aside, I submit the following simply for clarity. Contrary to what you may have heard Jim Griffin proclaim from the steps of the South Carolina appellate court last September (2023), this division happened, by *our* request, for comfort's sake. This was not the result of some diabolical plan hatched by a court official. We were not divided by gender, or anything else for that matter, including party politics and even shoe color. No one ever assigned us to a designated room.

I was particularly taken by a trial regular, who we'd see daily while people watching from our jury room window. His mere presence commanded attention. A man of average stature, he did not loom over the maddening crowd, but his beliefs sure did. Rev. Raymond Johnson, a National Civil Rights Activist and pastor from Mt. Pisgah Baptist Church in Marion, South Carolina, strolled among the gathered mob carrying what I can best describe as a picket sign. From our room with a view, I could not read the various placards he carried. It was not until I rewatched the trial and began researching this captivating figure that I learned his message(s). Written in large red lettering against a stark white background were powerful pronouncements, which included: Murdaugh Guilty; Justice Coming Soon; Praying for Everyone. In earnest supplication, with pleas for justice, Rev. Johnson often led trial watchers in prayer circles.

His black clerical vestment was accented by a shiny gold cross and white scarf embellished with blue crosses. Friends who attended the trial (and subsequent hearings) often commented on his huge, warm smile and genuine kindness that could ease the most anxious of souls. One can even boast of being Rev. Johnson's bench mate a couple of times. In fact, she was sitting with him when Creighton Waters was about to begin his cross-examination of Alex. AG Wilson returning from lunch, hurried past us in the gallery, Rev. Johnson extended his hand and said, "I'm praying for you and the team." To which the Attorney General responded, "Thank you. We need it." Saddened I was unable to catch up with him to learn the actual *why* behind his pervasive presence in the trenches of Murdaugh World, social media fed my basic curiosity, in a post that read, "As a minister of God, sometimes we must come from behind the pulpit and do like Jesus did. Get on foot patrol to do God's will to stand up for justice when justice is due." But what was driving his untiring commitment to this case? Joyce Orlando and Michael Dewitt caught up with him after the verdict was delivered, telling the *Greenville News* reporters, "Justice is here. He (Murdaugh) needs an Academy award for his performance (in the court), but he could not outperform God ... A Daddy is supposed to protect his wife and children, you aren't supposed to hurt your wife and child." Alex committed the ultimate betrayal, leaving Buster with the toughest cross to bear.

At long last, we would be permitted to talk to each other about topics which did not include our families, the weather, football, or what celebrity was spotted in the gallery. We had walked this path together and no other persons saw the gruesome, agonizing things we did. It was time to release six weeks of pent-up emotion and unpack any burning questions which remained. We could finally discuss what we believed happened to Maggie and Paul at

Moselle on that hot summer night. We were the designated finders of fact. I knew what the truth of the matter meant to me and
could defend my stance with evidence. What were my fellow jurors thinking? Did the testimony take them in the same direction
it took me? In just a few minutes, I would have answers to the
random questions that seemed to plague me in these final hours.
Judge Newman concluded his charge by saying:

> Madam forelady and members of the jury, I am required to
> charge you the law as I have done through these instructions
> now being given to help guide you to a just and lawful ver-
> dict. Remember you have no friends to reward or enemies to
> punish and all parties are entitled to a fair and impartial tri-
> al. Remember that although the foreperson is the only juror
> who writes the verdict it is not hers alone; the verdict must be
> unanimous. Madam forelady you are not authorized to write
> the verdict until all of you have agreed on it.

It was reported that we went back into the jury room around
3:35 on the afternoon of March 2, with the world officially beginning "verdict watch" at 3:50." Once court staff made sure we
had everything we needed, they left, locking the door behind
them. We settled into our seats, the forewoman began by saying, "It has been a long day; we don't have to do this tonight.
We all agreed to start deliberations and see where the discussion
led. In the meantime, while working toward the same common
goal—achieving justice for Maggie and Paul—our basic needs
were covered by an endless buffet of snacks, bottled water, and

coffee. Judge Newman could not have chosen a better person to direct our group; his years of courtroom experience obviously gave him a keen sense to recognize the leader among such a diverse group.

We began our deliberation process with an anonymous poll just to assess where everyone stood before putting forth our questions and reviewing evidence, which due to its abundance kept secured next door in Jury Room *B*. We began with an informal poll. Madame forewoman asked we respond to the central question, "Is he guilty?" We were to write Y=Yes (he is guilty); N=No (he is not guilty). The initial results were not unanimous with nine of us returning Y's; there were two N's, and one not sure.

After understanding everyone's stance, she opened the floor to questions. Remember, we were not allowed to take notes throughout testimony, but permitted to do so during a recess. Most, if not all, of my questions were answered as witness testimony continued. And others immediately looked to their notebooks for guidance during this part of deliberations.

I said it once, and it warrants repeating, Judge Newman recognized exactly what we needed and chose the perfect forewoman for this jury. She wanted to ensure that everyone felt like their voice would be heard and wanted to make sure that all the jurors felt comfortable sharing their areas of confusion, so *no one* would feel embarrassed or reticent to talk. Before we even got started, I can say, with certainty, among the twelve of us, intimidation was not in our vocabulary. Each of us felt like we were in a safe space, and our forewoman validated the importance of any opinion we might want to share before anyone even opened their mouth. As a result of her exemplary leadership, everyone spoke in a respectful tone, absent of condescension—no one glared with a haughty look of derision, raised their voice in frustration, or stomped their foot in anger. Everyone asked wonderful questions, that led us to review some key evidence, including, but not limited to interview footage, photos, and bullets.

Once this process was complete, our forewoman led us in a second informal poll to see if this stage of deliberations moved the needle in _either_ direction, be it toward Alex Murdaugh's innocence or his guilt. The results showed that our discussion clarified the facts of evidence. Madam forelady double-checked and triple checked that all questions were answered, and everyone was certain of their verdict. Reminding us to, "Make certain you are certain." She continued, "A man's life is at stake. This is not a game; there are no take backs. You must live with this; so, once again, make certain you are certain." I think we all appreciated her fervor in treating this verdict with the same insistence and care that might be expected in a death penalty case. Before advancing her pen to sign the first indictment, she gave one more reminder, "The decision does not have to be made tonight. If you are too anxious, tired, or just uncomfortable with the choice you made, we are under no time constraints. We can begin afresh tomorrow. It is vital that we remain true to our oath and arrive at a verdict which corresponds to the evidence." Unanimously, we reassured her that this was our real and true belief and that we were ready to bring forth the verdicts.

Our forewoman, with pen in hand, ready to sign verdict #1, had a look of partial relief, that seemed to welcome both the trial's end and a return to normalcy. However, her eyes emanated a bit of sorrow, not for Alex, but for his loved ones, his victims and their families who are left to suffer perpetually for his egregious misdeeds. With cautious deliberation, as instructed, she wrote our verdicts and signed her name:

Count # 1: Indictment for Murder—Guilty

Count #2: Indictment for Murder—Guilty

Count #3: Indictment for Possession of a Weapon during the Commission of a Violent Crime—Guilty

Count #4: Indictment for Possession of a Weapon during the Commission of a Violent Crime—Guilty

The culmination of our six weeks' worth of on-the-job training, coupled with seventy-six witnesses, almost six hours of closing arguments, and a five-star rebuttal sat right there in black-and-white before our eyes. Then just like that, the justice bus returned safely to the depot, signaling a new day to the citizens of South Carolina's Fourteenth Judicial Circuit and reminding us—*nobody* is above the law.

CHAPTER 11:
SIGNED, SEALED, DELIVERED

There is no word or phrase to describe how it felt watching our forelady meticulously examine the verdict sheets. She read through everything with great precision before putting an indelible mark next to the word "Guilty." Stopping shy of the signature line on each indictment, there was a noticeable shift in her gaze, reviewing the earlier sections to ensure the proper verdict had—indeed—been clearly checked. This should not be mistaken as a pause of doubt or hesitation, rather it was a reflection on the gravity of a task with no discernable room for error. Our forewoman understood her John Hancock carried the heft of twelve people and represented a consensus view on the defendant's guilt. It, too, proclaimed the remarkable conclusion of *our* truth seeking and fact-finding, by which *all* the evidence would end up pointing in the direction of one person—and one person only—Richard Alexander Murdaugh.

We perused the documents one final time, while audible sighs of relief made their way around our conference table, signaling sheer exhaustion and the end of our juror era (or so we thought). Madame forelady rose, then gave her chair a slight push backward before advancing toward the door to offer a knock which would inform the bailiff that we, the jury, had reached a verdict. I'm not sure why some people acted surprised that deliberations did not extend into Friday. Many inferred something was afoot in the jury room once we declined a dinner order. That rat-tat-tat echoed throughout the Colleton County Courthouse and beyond, causing quite a kerfuffle. It sent Nancy Grace bounding from the courtroom toward her media tent to change into a blazer. Similarly, journalists and VIPs poured from the media center, some anxious to claim their seat in the gallery, while others hurried to freshen up before going live at a moment's notice. Content creators, especially those who streamed the trial daily, sped to prepare their platforms for Thursday's impromptu second episode. Millions of at home trial watchers faced a conundrum—Court TV or Law & Crime. Once the difficult decision was made, they melted into their La-Z-Boys, where many would remain until the wee hours consuming every bit of post-verdict coverage. Between "court potatoes" sending text messages in rapid succession and posting on social media, it is a miracle there was not a cellular meltdown which spanned the globe.

I don't recall much being said while we waited for the bailiff to come in and say Judge Newman sounded his battle cry, "Bring the jury." I suppose we were lost in our own thoughts—wondering what Alex's demeanor might be when the verdict was read. Would he be stoic? Would he cry? Would his brothers, sister, or son have a vocalized reaction like some families on Court TV? And the real question was this, what would Dick do? Jim, I felt could exercise self-control, Dick, not so much. The wait was over. It was finally "go time." We reflexively lined up in the usual order, readying ourselves to enter the courtroom as "Alex's jury" one final time. When the doors of justice swung open, we walked into the loudest deafening silence I have ever heard. The crowd in the gallery seemed to have thinned out some since we retreated to begin deliberations. I learned later this was most likely due to the widespread confidence that the world would remain on verdict watch well into the weekend, if not beyond. Nonetheless, we could still feel the powerful leer of spectators and media closely watching us file into the courtroom. The only eyes not affixed in our direction were those of the family. Their vacuous stone-faced stares mirrored one another. For probably the first time in their lives, they were defenseless and incapable of controlling the outcome of a case. Gigi McKelvey observed, "The family looked super nervous, as did Alex whose movements seemed a bit jerky."

When facing the jury box from the courtroom floor, my seat was the last one in the second row. I walked that walk dozens of times in the preceding weeks, but this seemed surreal—almost personal. It was sobering to be in this unique position, where the entirety of a room looked to me—to us—for a simple answer to their complex question, "Will Maggie and Paul get the justice they deserve?" This time my chair seemed to be a distant mirage I might never reach. Everything was moving in slow motion. My shoes even felt like they were filled with concrete, making it difficult to put one foot in front of the other.

I kept my gaze forward, so as not to accidentally catch anyone's eye. While I never thought to ask my fellow jurors how they felt in the moments leading up to the unveiling of *our* verdict, I imagine they had similar feelings. The wait time between hearing those four magic words, "You may be seated" and the reading of the first verdict could not have been any more than two minutes, and I assure you, those were the longest one hundred twenty seconds I've ever experienced. To help put this in perspective, think back to Agent Rudofski's cross-examination for a second. Remember how Phil Barber set a timer for twenty seconds, demonstrating how that was plenty of time for Alex to "tend to Paul" and "tend to Maggie." When all it seemed to prove to us was that he had plenty of time to go to each body and make certain "it was official; they're dead." Multiply how long those twenty seconds felt to you by about one thousand and you'll understand what it means to be suspended in time.

As mentioned earlier, I had no idea what to expect from anyone in the courtroom—especially Alex—while the verdict was being read. I watched him intently, yet somehow remain clueless as to his true reaction. He stood inert with zero evidence of emotion showing on his face. That face—that face which showed such excessive emotion day-after-day as it tried to convince us of his innocence.

Flanked by Dick and Jim and surrounded by security officers and bailiffs, the defendant was told to rise to hear the verdict. Totally devoid of emotion, his posture was rigid; his soulless black eyes transfixed straight ahead directly on Judge Newman. Where was the swaying, sobbing, snotting, grief-stricken husband and father who sat in court for six weeks? Where were the protestations of a guiltless man who was just as much a victim as his only living son?

Judge Newman asked, "Madame Forelady, have you reached a verdict?" She replied, "Yes sir, we have." We were about to hear our verdict out loud for the first time. The former Clerk of Court stood at the front of the room and began:

Count # 1: Indictment for Murder—Guilty

Count #2: Indictment for Murder—Guilty

Count #3: Indictment for Possession of a Weapon during the Commission of a Violent Crime—Guilty

Count #4: Indictment for Possession of a Weapon during the Commission of a Violent Crime—Guilty

This marked the official end to our civic duty; then the formalities began to unfold. Judge Newman said, "Madame Forelady and members of the jury if that is the verdict of each and every juror, please let it be known by raising your right hand." He asked the defense if there was an individual polling requests to which

Dick, almost breathless, said "Yes." Gigi McKelvey, Host of *Pretty Lies and Alibis*, said the family was looking directly at us when the polling was happening. I was listening for my juror number and thinking how grateful I was that our forewoman mentioned this likelihood. I much preferred to be informed of the possibilities and not blindsided. In my previous stint as juror, polling was not requested, and I don't recall this ever happening on *Law and Order*. Had she unintentionally forgotten Judge Newman told her this might happen, several of us would have been puzzled, wondering what Dick and Jim thought we had done wrong—instead, they waited for almost six months to do that.

During the polling process, the former Clerk of Court called out each of our juror numbers one-by-one asking, "Is this your verdict? Is this still your verdict?" Once we all said "yes; yes." Jim then made a motion for a mistrial, as I have since learned is customary. In the moment I was thinking, "Are you kidding me?" Even-toned as always, Judge Newman denied their request and set sentencing for the following day. Alex was remanded into the custody of the Colleton County Sherriff's Department. Gigi noted two things I could not hear or see from the jury box. She mentioned how loud it was when the bailiff popped the handcuffs before placing them on Alex. She told her listeners there was no reason to believe it was done intentionally, but rather it showcased the deafening silence of the courtroom, as well as the solemnity of the moment. Secondly, as Alex turned around, he locked eyes with Buster when she saw him mouth something to his remaining son, what she believed to be, "It's okay; I love you" adding that Alex had tears in his eyes. With those five words, the only thing that mattered was Maggie and Paul finally got the justice they deserved.

Indifferent, unsympathetic, resolute, wooden are a few words tossed about in describing his reaction. The same can be said for the family, at least as I saw it from my vantage point. In witnessing the emotion, or rather lack thereof, exhibited by Alex and his brood, I can only discern strains of robot must run deep in the Murdaugh lineage. I only assume this is the authentic Richard Alexander Murdaugh—a heartless, callous, savage sociopath—who "loved Maggie and loved Paul but loved himself more." The untrained eye may have noticed a faint bristling in his overall demeanor as our findings were read aloud. However, body language expert Janine Driver noticed a subtle, yet telling, change in his facial movements explaining:

> The second and third time he was found guilty, he did an odd lip compression, pulling them down and then up. Historically we saw this when former governor of New York, Eliot Spitzer, gave his resignation speech amidst a prostitution scandal. We often see this when someone gets caught. This movement, a non-verbal expression, is their inward way of saying, "I made a huge mistake."

It cannot be denied—the body keeps the score. And Alex's body was jockeying for MVP, betraying him time-after-time and in the moments it mattered most. Throughout the investigation and trial, his consistently put points on the board in rapid succession. This was evident in Daniel Greene's body worn camera footage from June 7, 2021; his multiple interviews with David Owen; his fourteen hours of testimony, continuing through to sentencing. Shortly after the verdict was announced, *News Nation* asked Lillian Glass, another specialist in body language, what nonverbal cues she may have observed:

Head Nod: He was stoic for the few moments, and when he heard the first guilty, his head moved up and down, as if to say, "Yeah; I agree."

Jaw Clenching: When his name was mentioned there was tension in his jaw area; it's like reality set in.

Coloring: His color was very red during the trial, again his autonomic nervous system was in full gear. Here his complexion was even, and less red. Body Language speaks volumes for what's going on in his head.

I could not help but wonder how the Internet viewed our verdict. I poured through well over one hundred entries, with every user in agreement, "we got it right." I stated at the beginning of this memoir that—for better or worse—I was not afraid of the Murdaugh legacy; my job was to follow the evidence and so I did, although there seemed to be a slight divide among some users:

@Abbythelibb: AM found guilty of murdering his wife and son after only three hours of deliberations. Holy smokes! I really did not think that they would get justice.

@Meme_Streaker: He fooled no one! The closing arguments were longer than the jury's deliberation!

@mr_seans: I am not surprised. Dude couldn't find the truth with a map and compass.

@TheEricBland: This was not going to be an OJ Simpson jury. This was a jury that listened to the evidence and really understood that power and privilege was on trial as much as Alex Murdaugh.

@KBSpangler: What the What? They were expecting two full days of deliberations. This jury was riding the Alex Murdaugh train to guilty town.

@ImJohnEli: I'm so happy to eat my words about Alex Murdaugh! I would've bet anything that a good ole boy on the jury would have tried to free him. How fast was that jury verdict!

First and foremost, I appreciate the wit and insight provided by the real trial watchers of the Internet. I was surprised by the legitimate worry that we would fall prey to the underhanded trickery which kept the citizens of Hampton County (and surrounding areas) in-check—a few of which include:

1) A silent fear of the Murdaugh Mafia which held an anaconda-like grip on the Lowcountry for decades.

2) A two-tiered system of justice in which *Tier One* is Richard Alexander Murdaugh and *Tier Two* is every other person residing in the Fourteenth Judicial Circuit.

3) Serving on a pre-rigged jury, a "strategy" that Mark Tinsley implied was often employed by Alex to great success.

4) Southern Justice/The Good Ole Boys Club. This is steeped in two factors—legacy wealth and male privilege. It once worked for Alex many times over. Considering this went to trial, it can be deemed a failed tactic, as typically "Good Ole Boys" never see the inside of a courtroom.

The reactions of legal pundits, analysts, as well as a few other famous faces, focused on our "brief" deliberation time. Some expected it would be short, while others were astonished it did not continue for days. They were expressing an opinion based on experience and were in no way implying anything untoward happened in the jury room—Jim and Dick would do that months after the verdict was returned:

Ashley Banfield (News Nation): I am shocked at this verdict. I lived through OJ, whose deliberation was under 4 hours—after nine months of trial and ended in an acquittal. I thought there was plenty of reasonable doubt, and I thought that there was good evidence to prosecute, but, again, there was *a lot* of reasonable doubt.

Dan Abrams: This was a quick one, back in under three hours. It was clearly not even a close call for the jurors. I did not expect it would be this easy. At times the motive seemed muddled, but in a murder case motive does not have to be proven. Any uncertainty around the why apparently didn't make the case any harder for the jury in determining what had happened.

Jesse Weber: I just said on air that I thought it would be a hung jury. I thought they were going to wrestle with this into the next week. However, if I could only predict guilt or acquittal, I would say guilty. He had long explanations of everything: why he lied, why he sped to Almeda, why he said or did not say things to key players. I think the jury said none of this makes sense, right? I was surprised at the speed but not necessarily the outcome.

Carl B. Grant (Legal Analyst/Attorney): The verdict was resounding. It was unanimous; it was decisive; and it was swift. So this tells you the jurors thought the evidence was strong, very strong. I've told jurors this many times in opening statements, when you came here, you parked your cars, but you did not park your common sense. And that is what they used to come to the decision; based upon what—evidence.

Judge Newman (when asked if he was surprised by the verdict's speed): I wasn't. It has been my experience in recent years that jurors don't take a long time deliberating after they've spent weeks and weeks and weeks listening to testimony and receiving evidence.

OJ Simpson (Yes, that OJ Simpson): A whole lot of people are asking me about this Alex Murdaugh trial. I don't know why they think I'm an expert on it. He was just trying to relate to one or two of those jurors that he was a good ole boy. It wouldn't surprise me in the least if this guy beats this case.

This trial had everything. We had Covid, a bomb threat, a dozen eggs, all with a side of OJ. Of course, I did not know that "The Juice" chimed in on Alex's guilt or innocence until months after the verdict when I stumbled upon the video posted by X user **@ ted_clfrd**, with a caption that read, "The Murdaugh jury began their deliberations at 3:50. They have been instructed not to view outside media, which is a shame because they could use some pointers from noted legal scholar OJ Simpson." All I can say is it is a good thing he decided to become a professional athlete and career criminal, rather than attend law school.

Then Judge Newman said, "And he may be taken away." The newly convicted murderer was led from the courtroom by two members of the Colleton County Sheriff's office in front and a policeman not too far behind. That was the first time he had ever walked past us, and the last time he would wear khakis and a button-down shirt. That was the first time we sat in the jury box, knowing the ending of the story (or so we thought), and the last night he would spend in county lock-up before heading to prison. That was also the first time we, the jury, were shown on television.

Once the family annihilator was escorted away, Judge Newman spoke directly to us, offering us his genuine, wholehearted gratitude and sharing some sage wisdom:

On behalf of the citizens of the state of South Carolina and your fellow citizens of Colleton County you did not volunteer for this service you were called upon by summons to appear. Providence that brought you to this moment in time. I know that all of you have been here at a great sacrifice. I want to thank each one of you all individually and collectively. It's not often that you're called upon to sit in judgment of the actions of your fellow man. You all gave due consideration to the evidence. I will make no comment now as to the extent or the overwhelming nature of the evidence but certainly the verdict that you've reached supported by the circumstantial evidence, direct evidence, all of the evidence, pointed to only one conclusion. That's the conclusion you reached. I applaud you for evaluating the evidence and coming to a proper conclusion as you saw the facts of the case.

That was the perfect speech to end such an exhausting day. When I finally returned to my vehicle that evening, I anticipated having a couple of missed calls or texts, from the few people who knew how I'd spent the last six weeks. Nevertheless, it was my best friend who would send me the most shocking text of all—a video she'd recorded from her television screen showing how a court camera panned the length of the entire jury box. It seemed one of the videographers became a bit too excited by Alex's perp walk from the courtroom. I was shocked but could not summon any sort of reaction, be it ire or indifference. I was, however, distressed for my fellow jurors who had no intention of speaking to the media.

I pointed my Jeep in the direction of home. The paved roads seemed infinite, each one stretching before the next in a never-ending line. I could not help but think of my family who I could see, touch, talk to without the constraints of designated visiting hours or phone privileges, nor would a pane of glass separate parent from child. Once home, I thought about my fellow jurors. We were twelve strangers six weeks ago, and now we were family. I let exhaustion win, knowing the gang of twelve—well, ten of us anyway—would be reunited one final time tomorrow (or so I thought).

As hard as Dick and Jim worked to step into "Handsome's" role as Alex's personal clean-up crew and "fixer," it was not happening with this jury. I am certain social media trolls will take that statement straight to the spin room and feast on it with a nice Chianti and some fava beans, claiming this as proof he never had a chance at a fair trial. To which my only reply is, "It's better to be silent and thought a fool than to speak and remove all doubt." By following the evidence—all that evidence—we escaped from Alex's labyrinth of lies to attain justice for Maggie and Paul.

CHAPTER 12:
LIFE IN PRISON

Waking before my phone's ill-mannered alarm began its daily clamor, I had a curious sensation. It took me a minute to identify the peculiar feeling. Then whammo—it suddenly struck me. I was unburdened and worry free for the first time since January 23, 2023.

The darkness of night gradually yielded the new day's dawn to a sky empty of clouds, revealing Divine promise the day (March 3, 2023) would be filled with abundant sunshine—in both the literal and figurative sense. Just a few hours prior, Alex Murdaugh's standing within the criminal justice system was reclassified. His status of alleged murderer, cloaked in a robe of innocence, was quickly converted to his forever rank of convicted murderer, outfitted in a prison issued jumpsuit. This demotion offered assurance, across five counties, that sunshine would soon emerge from the dismal, dense fog which obscured the area's legal landscape for decades.

In contrast, it was my inaugural reentry into the role I surrendered six weeks earlier. Less than twenty-four hours ago, I handed over my juror number in return for my name and station in life—Amie Williams, ordinary citizen. An oath of silence was replaced by a barrage of zealous media, anxious to listen to anything I (and my fellow jurors) had to say. Then, in a few short days, I would resume my position as a payroll specialist.

I sank into the recliner; coffee in one hand and remote control in the other. Trying to recall my latest Netflix binge, I paused, then snapped back into reality. I could, once again, spend mornings with Savannah, Craig, Al, and Hoda. *The Today Show* was no longer jurors' forbidden fruit. In fact, the moratorium on all television programs vaporized the second deliberations ended. Excited to see what was going on in the world, I also scrolled through a few online newspapers. Regretfully, it seemed Alex Murdaugh's verdict was the only newsworthy current event on the planet. Countless headlines read much like the following:

The New York Times: "Alex Murdaugh Convicted of Murdering Wife and Son" (Nicholas Bogel-Burroughs)

The Week: Daily Briefing: "South Carolina Jury Finds Disgraced Lawyer Alex Murdaugh Guilty of Murder"

APNews: "Jury Quickly Finds Alex Murdaugh Guilty of Murdering Wife and Son"

NewsNation: "Alex Murdaugh Found Guilty of Killing Wife and Son" (Sean Noone and Tyler Wornell)

ABC7NY: "Murdaugh Murders: Disgraced South Carolina Attorney Found Guilty in Double Murder of Wife and Son" (Meredith Deliso)

This ubiquitous coverage did not come as a complete shock to me. After all, we did share the courtroom with loads of media whose focus orbited Murdaugh World—before, during, and after the double murder trial. To see our verdict reported as a matter of fact and without spin was a blessing. Crickets were the only thing that could be heard from Alex's pocket-sized coterie of supporters. Despite having delivered a just and unanimous verdict, we would soon find ourselves trapped in the eye of Hurricane Alex (and his tornadic defense team).

Ten deliberating jurors told the bailiff they wanted to attend Alex's sentencing. They first briefed us on our designated parking area, located not too far from the courthouse grounds. Secondly, we were instructed to remain in place until our security detail arrived. Members of SLED and the Colleton County Sherriff's Office would escort us to a meeting room where we could chat and wait for court to begin. Maintaining total professionalism, and talking about anything other than the verdict, we exchanged pleasantries. One even asked, "So who do you guys want to play ya'll in the movie?" None of us considered the thought. In the end, we were just faceless men and women who had been court ordered to be kept out of camera range (apart from the previous night's faux pas). Only hearing a couple of responses, I piped up with the same answer I've given for years when this question is bandied about during church, work or conference ice breakers, proclaiming, "I want Halle Berry to play me!"

We were led to a side entrance hidden within a small court-yard. Its iron rod fence was shrouded in leafy green tendrils that would soon blossom in the plush aromas of jasmine. The flower-ing vine crept along each wall, snaking in and out—out and in—of every spindle which helped provide an extra layer of privacy. This area cloistered entrants from a crowd of curious onlookers and gave some added distance between the media and any jurors who preferred to remain anonymous. It's strange to think this remote entryway was strategically chosen to shield us from the masses, yet it was a honey hole for paparazzi who assembled in wait for Alex's morning and afternoon perp walk.

Once in the courthouse, we instinctually began walking in the direction of the jury room. However, security diverted us toward an area that housed personnel offices, with an unoccupied room reserved specifically for jurors—correction, former jurors. Some-one jokingly said, "Ahh, so it wasn't a dream after all; we are no longer members of the jury." Before court was slated to begin, a few visitors stopped by to extend their appreciation. Among them were the human lie detector and SLED's lead investigator, David Owen; telemetry data decoder and timeline wunderkind,

Peter Rudofski; and trial superstar, crime scene reconstructionist, Dr. Kenny Kinsey. Each wanted to make sure they had the opportunity to extend their personal gratitude and say, "thank you for your service." That was a surprise. They did the hard work of running the investigation, compiling the data, and analyzing the crime scene. Their heavy lifting made it easy for us to deliver swift justice. It will be a while before I forget how genuinely moved Dr. K was when we thanked him for his straightforward account of what happened at Moselle on the night of June 7, 2021. In one of Dr. Kinsey's first post-trial interviews, he commented, "I'm generally a fairly tough guy, but that reached all the way to my soul. I don't think you can ask for anything better, and I was so humbled because I just wanted to drop down and thank them for sacrificing that much of their life for their civic duty." Hearing this interview was heartwarming and a true testimonial to who he is both personally and professionally.

The bailiff said we would enter and exit the courtroom as a group, via the same entranceway we used as jurors. He also informed us our reserved seating in the gallery was located on the prosecution's side and a few rows behind the media. While waiting for Judge Newman to enter, I surveyed the room one last time. The Murdaugh family, save for Randy, maintained their perfect attendance record. Staring straight ahead the entire time, not one of them appeared to scan their surroundings in search of a familiar, supportive face in the crowd, nor did anyone break their stony gaze to side-eye our rows. None of us expected any sort of silent acknowledgement—good, bad, or indifferent— from the family. Please don't misconstrue this as an insult to the

Murdaughs or contort it into a statement claiming the jury has a hero complex. Even without an undertaker, floral arrangements, and a few verses of "Amazing Grace," this may as well have been Alex's funeral. He was *never* returning home. Each family member was grieving an individual loss for a father, brother, and uncle who they will always love and support.

Then I turned my eyes toward the empty jury box and reflected on the many atrocities we heard and were supposed to—in one way or another—make sense of. Just thinking about Alex Murdaugh's abysmal depravity was repulsive. However, it was not the time to dwell on his hideous behavior. This day marked the triumphant conclusion to his reign of terror. The twelve of us may have slain the monster, but we could not have done it without the help of countless members of Maggie and Paul's justice league, *some* of whom include, but are not limited to, law enforcement, Creighton Waters, his team, and Kenny Kinsey.

While it was a sorrow-filled day for Alex's family, it was a brand-new era for countless others. It was one free from fear and teeming with renewed promise. I hope the Branstetter and Proctor families at least saw a tiny glimmer of light penetrate through the immeasurable darkness which has consumed them day-after-day and night-after-night since June 7, 2021. With the knowledge Alex will be spending two lifetimes in prison for savagely murdering Maggie and Paul, I pray they give themselves permission to begin the healing process.

Overnight, the convicted murderer swapped his business casual for a khaki one-piece jumpsuit with CCJ emblazoned on the back in large, black lettering. He relinquished his dark slip-on tennis shoes for some fluorescent orange shower slides which appeared even brighter against the white crew socks he was sporting. His restraints were more elaborate than the single pair of cuffs he regularly tried to disguise by draping a sportscoat betwixt his bound hands. At sentencing, Alex's handcuffs were attached by a long silver chain to the leg irons clutching his ankles. This 3-piece restraint ensemble made a jingling sound when he walked, thus heralding his entrance into the courtroom. Led in by various members of law enforcement, Alex showed off his mastery of the convict shuffle as he lumbered and rattled across the well to the defense table.

The bailiff's roar of, "All rise. Court is now in session. Judge Newman presiding. Be seated" echoed throughout the courtroom. The first order of business was to inquire if anyone was present to make a victim's impact statement. *No one* chose to speak—not even Buster who was doing double duty as a staunch supporter of his father *and* as a victim of his father's heartless, murderous ire. I'm sure it surprised no one when Alex Murdaugh triumphantly seized his right to allocution, allowing him one last chance to make millions of trial watchers cringe upon hearing Paul called "Paw-Paw." I confess—I could not roll my eyes hard enough[1] when he uttered that overdone nickname or the meaningless refrain, "I'm innocent. I would never hurt my wife Maggie, and I would never hurt my son Paw-Paw. Thank you, your Honor." Body Language analyst Janine Driver maintained his use of minimizing language at sentencing gave a more compelling indication of his guilt than any subtleties in his nonverbal communication:

In training FBI, CIA, and Scotland Yard police we have learned when people declare 'I'm innocent,' they are in fact guilty. Instead of saying, 'I did not murder,' or 'I did not kill,' he gave a weak denial when it mattered the most. Tense shifts happen frequently with the guilty; we heard this with Susan Smith who spoke in the past tense when she said, 'I loved my kids.' In Alex's case, he used the future tense, 'I would never hurt Maggie and I would never hurt Paw-Paw. Of course, he would not hurt them—they are dead.

In addition, Driver notes she saw two telling elements in his body language. First his consistent tongue protrusions indicate an increase in stress and cognitive thinking. Secondly, he had a lot of eye fluttering which suggested an emotional struggle, especially when he spoke about Maggie and Paul.

Knowing Judge Newman's respect for the rule of law, I anticipated he would have a few harsh words for Alex, before handing down his sentence. Drew Tripp, of *Unsolved South Carolina* said, "Judge Newman wanted his pound of flesh, and he got it. He was tearing him apart. It sounded almost medieval." With measured tone, Judge Newman began to excoriate the fallen legal scion:

This is particularly troubling, Mr. Murdaugh, you are a well-known member of the legal community and have practiced law before me. We have seen each other on many occasions throughout the years. It has been especially heartbreaking for me to see you go, in the media, from grieving father and husband to the person being indicted then convicted of murdering them. You have engaged in such duplicitous conduct here in the courtroom, here on the witness stand, you have no obligation to say anything other than saying not guilty.

Alex did not even flinch at these acerbic words. To hear this revered, kind jurist sound so personally and profoundly wounded by a former colleague's heinous actions was painful. Mark Fava, known to his blog followers as "aviator lawyer" commented, "The judge's sentencing sounded like an incredibly disappointed father figure. Compassionate, yet direct. Highly impactful, yet soft spoken. For almost 20 minutes Judge Newman methodically addressed Murdaugh." Choosing each word carefully, he made certain Alex did not forget his family's notoriety when it came to pursuing the death penalty:

In this case, it qualifies under our death penalty statute based on the statutory aggravating circumstances of two or more people being murdered by the defendant by one act or pursuant to one scheme or one course of conduct. I don't question at all the decision of the state not to pursue the death penalty. But as I sit here in the courtroom and look around at the many portraits of judges and other court officials and reflect on the fact that over the past century, your family, including you, have been prosecuting people in this courtroom and many have received the death penalty, probably for lesser conduct.

Alex showed no emotion. No sorrow for his murdered wife and son. No remorse for his despicable crimes. No gratitude for the state's refusal to pursue the death penalty. Judge Newman would reference this deadpan interaction later at a subsequent hearing, calling Alex "empty," and saying, "I don't see anything." His remarks concluded with words that would sting anyone and anything with a heart; however, the hollow man in the khaki prison issued jumpsuit remained emotionless:

I can just imagine on that day June 7th when a lawyer is confronted and confesses to having stolen over half a million dollars from a client, and he has a tiger like Mark Tinsley on his tail pursuing the death of Mallory Beach and having a father for the most part on his deathbed, I can imagine, or I can't really imagine, but I know that it had to be quite a bit going through your mind on that day. But amazingly to have you come to testify that it was just another ordinary day that my wife and son and I were just out enjoying life. It is not credible. It is not believable. You can convince yourself about it, but obviously, you have the inability to convince anyone else about that. So, if you made any such arguments as a lawyer, you would lose every time, and cases that you will not have the opportunity to argue anymore, except perhaps your own as you sit in the Department of Corrections.

I clung to his every word, wondering what merited barb Judge Newman would launch next. His words spoke to the totality of Alex's criminal enterprise, as well as the multitude of victims he left floundering in the fallout. His wrongdoings began with thievery and ended in murder; this would be the day Alex learned his fate for the commission of what Judge Newman called "the most heinous crime known to man," and he held nothing back:

> All right. Mr. Murdaugh, I sentence you to the state Department of Corrections on each of the murder indictments in the murder of your wife Maggie Murdaugh. I sentence you for the term of your natural life. For the murder of Paul Murdaugh, whom you probably loved so much, I sentence you to prison for murdering him for the rest of your natural life. Those sentences will run consecutively. Under the statute involving a crime where there is no other involving indictment of other crimes, you are remanded to the Department of Corrections. And officers may carry forth on the imposition.

I've heard it said the British have such a beautiful accent they could read the ingredients on a soup can and somehow make it sound mesmerizing. Likewise, Judge Newman had a similar talent. He could publicly eviscerate a malignant narcissist, yet it would sound like a coach giving his star player a pep talk before the big game.

With staggering deference, Judge Newman "threw the book" at Alex, sentencing him to a double dose of LWOP (life without parole), as he so richly deserved. Then posthaste law enforcement transported the freshly minted lifer to Kirkland Correctional Institution, a maximum-security facility in Columbia, South Carolina. It took no time for Alex's updated mugshot to go viral. His striking new no maintenance haircut would mean he had more canteen money for honey buns and beef sticks. Shampoo and conditioner were now pointless. His bright yellow jumpsuit and smug grin drew attention to his soulless, beady, black eyes, which ultimately provided the complete portrait of a rabid egomaniac. Little did we know this photo was a warning that Team Murdaugh was already in the planning stages of their next diabolical scheme. However, Inmate 00390394 had to complete state mandated requirements before the trio could publicly unleash their vile plan.

As one of its many functions, Kirkland works as the intake center for SCDC's male inmates. WLTX explained the standard procedure Murdaugh experienced at the Columbia prison, "new transfers get an evaluation on a variety of aspects, including medical and mental health tests, education assessments, and other background appraisals. In addition, there is an inmate classification system that uses several metrics to determine where the inmate will spend the rest of their sentence and which custody level they need." Once the process is complete, they are reassigned to another maximum-security facility. News articles reported Alex completed the intake process sooner than the allotted 45-day period. It probably came as no surprise to trial watchers that Alex's initial transfer was nebulous and dramatic, with a red herring tossed in the mix for good measure. When he was ready to be transferred, the world played a round of "Where in SCDC is Alex Murdaugh." After a brief layover in an undisclosed location, he was transferred to his forever home, McCormick Correctional Institution. This facility provides Alex with "three hots and a cot" and likewise serves as the supervillain's evil lair, where he still seems to be relentlessly plotting the team's next move in their dangerous game of judicial whack-a-mole.

Judge Newman marked the official end of *SC* vs. *Richard Alexander Murdaugh* with a bam-bam of his gavel. The bailiff waited by the door to escort us out of the Colleton County Courthouse for the very last time. We exited through the same beautiful little enclosure as we entered. A throng of trial watchers, committed to giving the lifer a sendoff of leers and jeers, gathered just outside of its iron rod gates. Some cheers could even be heard when the jail van finally pulled from the curb, whisking him far from the Fourteenth Judicial Circuit for the rest of his natural life. I was pleased to see the Reverend Raymond Johnson, sign in hand, was still tarrying outside of the courtyard. When we filed out, he began to cheer, "Thank you! Thank you!" And then the rest of the crowd followed suit. That "fanfare," for lack of a better word, was not expected, but very much appreciated. From our window, we watched Rev. Johnson's signage evolve over the preceding six weeks, but the one he carried on March 3, 2023, spoke the most to me. It was proof positive; my jury service was blessed. The red and white placard he carried contained only one word—Justice. I can't think of any better person than the Rev. Raymond Johnson to hand deliver me this timely God wink, mere minutes after Maggie and Paul got the justice they deserved. After all, the blood of the unjustly killed cries out for vengeance, as scripture says, "And he said, what hast thou done? The voice of thy brother's blood crieth unto me from the ground" (Gen. 4:10).

EPILOGUE:
BACK TO LIFE
(BACK TO REALITY)

Alex Murdaugh effectively lost his life on March 3, 2023, after receiving two consecutive life sentences. In turn, it would be the day I began reclaiming my own life—right after I figured out how to navigate the media blitz. Having shared the courtroom with throngs of reporters, coupled with watching the coverage of many high-profile trials, it was a given we would be among the first asked for interviews. I wrestled with this possibility during the last week of trial and was not committed to speaking out or staying silent. I could see value in staying out of the public eye, and truthfully the thought of being on television kind of terrified me. Ultimately, I decided to trust that I would recognize my path when the time came.

Today reached out to the entire panel of deliberating jurors, with one producer calling me and another emailing. Of the twelve, only three of us accepted their invitation. We flew to New York. So often I am asked if we got paid for interviews; no, we did not. Do your fellow man a favor, if you see a troll feeding off jurors who chose to speak out, shut them down. It was a whirlwind

trip, but nonetheless exciting. We did two live interviews and recorded a segment for a future *Dateline* episode. It was wonderful to meet Craig, Hoda, and Savannah. At that point, it never occurred to me, I would still be speaking out about Alex Murdaugh ten months after the verdict. It is safe to say, at this point, if Craig happened to be visiting his hometown for the South Carolina State Fair and we ran into each other in the line for Fried Oreos, he would say, "Hey Amie! How's it going?"

Once I returned home, all my juror and Murdaugh duties were complete. It was time to focus on me, and the first item on my to-do list—call the dentist. Just before Presidents' Day, I started having tooth pain. Those who have experienced this in any capacity know it is not for the faint of heart. This is no exaggeration, when serious enough, one's entire face, including the sinus cavities may throb. If the problem progressed to the point of needing a root canal, the phantom heartbeat radiating from the tooth is loads of fun. As if having a filling fall out when the defense had only just begun their case-in-chief was not enough, the pain I was experiencing on the opposite side was not "referred pain," I needed a root canal. Dr. Wallace and her team of angels from Palmetto Smiles came to the rescue with prescription strength Motrin and the promise of getting me in promptly after the trial concluded. Between the non-drowsy pain reliever and careful eating, I was able to stay comfortable and focused for the remainder, and even a bit longer. Judge Newman, Kenny Kinsey, and countless others said, "Thank you for sacrificing so much of your time." I never thought about my service as a personal sacrifice, per say. However, looking back, postponing my dental work, another unrelated medical procedure, and knowing what my fellow jurors were going through, I understand exactly what they meant. While it was happening, my only thought was I had to get it figured out. I could not abandon Maggie and Paul. I was part of their justice league and had to see it through until the very end. That was my only option. The freedom of self-care, at least during traditional business hours, is virtually non-existent when jury service extends week-after-week, and in some cases months. Keeping a laundry list of what ifs is no way to live; nor will a judge, even one as kind as Judge Newman, accept hypotheticals as a viable reason for excusal from jury service.

I really enjoyed getting back into my workweek's grind and routine and never begrudged the curiosity of friends or strangers. That was, after all, what led me to put this experience on paper. It was much more pleasurable rewatching trial footage with a mute button right at my fingertips. Which reminds me of one thing I forgot to say earlier. Dick and Jim could replay it slow; they could replay it fast, or even through a Darth Vader voice changer, Alex said, "I did him so bad," and we all knew it!

PART II

"It is certain, in any case, that ignorance, allied with power, is the most ferocious enemy justice can have."

--James Baldwin

PREFACE II:
WILL YOUR LAWYER TALK TO GOD

Throughout six long weeks, beginning January 25, 2023, and concluding the morning of March 3rd, I heard endless hours of testimony related to the gruesome deaths of Paul and Maggie Murdaugh. This was the devastating crescendo in a layered tale of avarice with tentacles so far-reaching it would forever alter the lives of an array of innocent people. It never occurred to me that I, along with my fellow jurors, would be added to Alex's growing list of victims.

First, let's start with the players—Jim Griffin, Dick Harpoofetlian, and the often seen and occasionally heard from, Phillip Barber. Since the very beginning, these guys have made infinite protestations about the constant media coverage of their client, his family, and waxing public interest. That is indisputable. However, they don't hesitate to be self-serving attention mongers and talk (and talk) to espouse their greatest hits, such as, "We have new information on the real killers," and "Alex Murdaugh **_did not_** kill his wife and son. Yet, they are quick to claim reporters, both print and broadcast, are exploiting their client's family tragedy and financial misdeeds for the purposes of "clinging to fame." *Newsflash, Dick: your deputy attorney has his own podcast, and he will get in front of a microphone quicker than you can marginalize the people you once referred to as constituents.* Lastly, one of their favorite past times is to mock and demean Murdaugh Trial Watchers and True Crime Fans. However, they quickly packed their suitcases and headed to Orlando, Florida, for CrimeCon 2023. For those who may be unaware, this is exactly what it sounds like—an annual convention for true crime fans. Based on photos I saw from last year's event, the lines for their meet-and-greet had little to no waiting. Clearly hypocrisy is not in their vocabulary, nor do they have any shame. This was not meant to be a salty speech upon my soapbox but a framework for understanding their scorched earth "the ends justify the means" approach to representing Richard Alexander Murdaugh.

Moving on to the where; picture it, Columbia, South Carolina, 2023. It was a hot September afternoon when the Murdaugh crusaders took to a cluster of microphones each branded with the names of national and local news stations, all strategically positioned before an edifice symbolic of justice. Yet, it was there a massive injustice would occur. With the South Carolina Court of Appeals as their background, #Team2Shooters, #Team5ft2inVigilantes, and #TeamMaybetheWalterboroCowboys, lobbed false allegations of jury tampering. In an instant, we, the jury, were catapulted into a SLED investigation so steeped in disinformation that, to this day, I remain astounded a spontaneous five-alarm pants fire did not ensue before the steps of South Carolina's Court of Appeals.

Murdaugh's coterie threatened twelve people who did not ask for this responsibility but were *chosen*. Twelve people who were acting as civil servants. Twelve people who were getting paid $20.00 a day, some of whom were hourly employees and did not get a paycheck for six weeks. Twelve people who collectively carried the burden of deciding how their man would spend the remainder of his life. Each of us made peace with this incredible responsibility; however, we had NO idea that maintaining our integrity was contingent upon an acquittal for a double murderer, thereby putting a "W" in the defense column. I can honestly say, if a soothsayer had cautioned, "Hell hath no fury like a male ego scorned," we would have done nothing differently.

CHAPTER 1:
WHAT'S THE MATTER HERE

It took me no time to settle back into the routine—the normalcy—I had enjoyed for most of my adult life. Everything happened organically. Winter turned to Spring, then Spring turned to Summer. My son's sophomore year ended, and before we knew it, the hottest day on record had arrived, indicating college move-in day was upon us. After a few weeks, my Murdaugh obsessed friends turned their energy and focus to the ninety-nine financial crimes. Those who were local could not wait to see if a hearing would be in their backyard because truthfully there was equal parts interest in seeing Alex on trial—again—as well as watching Judge Newman retake the bench. I was just glad to have the autonomy to say, "No Thank you; have fun!" Because if Cirque de Murdaugh popped up on my TV screen, I could press mute or click "Not Interested in Alex Murdaugh" if I saw him on my Google homepage. Amie Williams—regular citizen—was living stress free and enjoying the excitement of a first book and starting a non-profit shelter (Sanctuary House) for domestic abuse victims. Then out of nowhere an extraordinary tempest began to rage and pose a direct threat to my ordinary life. Devoid of compunction, ringmaster Murdaugh alongside his two jesters, Dick and Jim, foist us into the center ring, where—we the jury—would be put on display as their showstopping spectacle. Due to this, it would unfortunately be a long while before Alex Murdaugh's name no longer entered my mouth at least twice a day.

The events surrounding Labor Day weekend (2023) remain etched in memory almost a year later, and thinking back on it, still elicits a visceral reaction from head-to-toe. I am so grateful that I missed Griffin's interview on News Nation's *Cuomo* which aired that Thursday leading into the holiday weekend. His appearance served as a save the date notice, in where he offered a vague cagey hint that something was afoot in Murdaugh World. Oozing with contempt he told the host and viewers, "there are serious questions as to whether this jury was subject to outside influences during the case . . . we have been diligently interviewing jurors and the information we have unearthed, so far, has, in my experience as a lawyer, been unprecedented." Had I been tuned in, I would have never been able to enjoy my three-day weekend—and a perfect one it was with a restful Saturday and a prayerful Sunday that rejuvenated my spirit. The best part was, I still had one more day left to enjoy. I was looking forward to a Monday that demanded very little of me. In fact, the only place I needed to be was in my recliner on Zoom for a meeting with Shana (my co-author) and Melissa (troll slayer, photographer, cover artist, sanity keeper). We were so excited to hammer out the details of our upcoming photoshoot with her and to discuss the pictures she was contributing to our book. She is incredibly talented and took amazing snapshots during the week she and her bestie attended Alex Murdaugh's double murder trial. Likewise, she had some amazing candids of the crowds as she stood in line, as well as ones of Alex taking his twice daily perp walk.

We talked about our friendship being a silver lining within the tragedy, a sentiment I heard shared by many others like Lauren Mathias (*Hidden True Crime*) and Gigi McKelvey (*Pretty Lies and Alibis*). This was such an exciting time for Shana and me; the book was underway, and we had an incredible photographer rowing the boat with us. As we waived goodbye on our Zoom call, I was going to indulge in an early afternoon slumber.

While I slept peacefully, word of a mysterious press conference had travelled from the Midlands to the Lowcountry, which in summary, read: "Richard Harpootlian and Jim Griffin, would be hosting a press conference on Tuesday, Sept. 5, at 2:30 p.m. on the south side of the South Carolina State House grounds, near the Court of Appeals, to discuss a newly filed motion for a new trial based on newly 'discovered evidence.'"

With Alex having more charges than Carter has pills, it was not initially clear about what evidence for what case they were referencing because surely—surely—they were not talking about the murder trial. However, one-half of Alex's legal power couple was the embodiment of what it means to be a showman and grandstander, so the location of the presser was symbolic. It was about his murder conviction. Melissa, Shana, and I started a group text; we each rooted around our individual social media accounts to see if anyone had anything to say—there was nothing. We poked around various news stations and newspapers—they were equally as clueless as the three of us. We spent a little time going back-and-forth with absolute speculation. Was there some archaic loophole they unearthed and believed could apply to the convicted family annihilator? No! No! They certainly did not plan to throw Judge Newman under the bus for some imagined and preposterous reason. Never once, not ever, and at no time, did I ever dream they would point Murdaugh's sinking ship straight into a raging tempest of their own making.

The long weekend did not end in such a way that made me ready to face the week. I was dreading the next day. In between ringing, my phone was lighting up with Facebook messages, texts, and e-mails from concerned friends and curious reporters. By sundown on Labor Day, news of the presser was making its way around the globe. I was mentally exhausted. After checking in with my parents and son, I silenced my phone and gave it to the Lord.

CHAPTER 2:
SOMETHING TO TALK ABOUT

Knowing Team Murdaugh was about to toss a hand grenade straight into the wheels of justice was unsettling, to say the least. The normalcy I enjoyed for the past six months was coming to an end. I just knew for an indefinite amount of time my world— and that of my fellow jurors—would be on a collision course with team Murdaugh. I could no longer tune out news cycles that centered around the ginger-haired menace. They did not call this presser to give a random update on the appeal they filed almost immediately after our verdict—just six months prior. The only thing we knew about the news conference was that it had some- thing to do with the murder conviction which meant somehow it was about us. How could it not be? Would their "explosive" announcement effectively silence the voice we gave to Maggie and Paul? I tried to enjoy a peaceful morning, but I could not escape Alex Murdaugh. His name and face were already on every channel and all-over social media,

The hours leading up to the big reveal felt interminable. I took a quick break and reached for my phone to see if there was any news, and I had three missed texts, each with screenshots. Initially I thought my friends were sending funny memes of support. That was not the case. Instead, they had all sent the same news brief. There were not any details, but they did offer one specific of what we could expect—claims of jury tampering. Of course, I was astonished. How could this even be possible? I was there every day for six weeks; I was a jury member. Nothing untoward happened. Just the notion of this left me speechless, and that seldom happens.

I tuned into the stream during my lunch break. Then as the trio ambled toward the podium, all suited up and decked out in their dapper sunglasses, with bravado spilling out of every orifice. Succinctly put, the Clerk of Court was Alex's sacrificial lamb, and we were their pawns. Amidst the chaos they were about to unleash, I spotted a God wink in the crowd. Standing in silent protest of Murdaugh World's latest assault on the judicial system was the Reverend Raymond Johnson holding a "Murdaugh Guilty" sign above his head.

Alex's defense team stood before the highest court in South Carolina claiming their client did not receive a fair trial. We, the jury, along with the former clerk of court, were now at the center of a full-throated attempt to get their client a new trial. Dick and Jim wove an elaborate tale of woe featuring Alex Murdaugh as the victim. The same Alex Murdaugh who took an oath to uphold our justice system, yet somehow, he was only able to ravish and exploit her—decade-after-decade. They were alleging an elected official worked behind the scenes to tip the scales of justice against Richard Alexander Murdaugh. They told the world the former clerk was so blinded by dollar signs and a desperation for fame she decided to write a book.

According to Alex's defense counsel, her success was contingent on one thing, and one thing only—a guilty verdict. They further argued, she launched a pre-meditated campaign of subliminal messaging to ensure we, the jury, would see things her way. After all, at the trial's end, the verdict would lay expressly in our hands. Had I not been so bowled over by these allegations, I might literally have been ROFL (rolling on the floor laughing).

I walked through every interaction we had with the former clerk, not one of them was troubling. After the shock wore off, I began to process what these accusations said about me—about us, the jury—then, I got mad. What Dick, Jim, and back-up minion, Phil just said on the world's stage was that we were gulled and manipulated into thinking Alex Murdaugh killed his wife and son. Then because of a devious outside influence we eagerly sold out, forfeiting our God given gift of free will **AND** our intelligence in support of the wanton desires of another. With the then clerk playing puppeteer, we bent to her whims, which rendered us incapable of upholding our sworn oath to 1) listen to evidence 2) apply the law 3) reach a verdict 4) follow instructions and 5) make sound arguments. Before I continue, please allow me to clarify one thing. This is not my view on the clerk's reasons for writing a book; it was my interpretation of the allegations made at the press conference and how we, the jury, fit into Murdaugh's grand plan.

Does any of what Team Murdaugh espoused sound like a *logical* way to get from murder conviction to mistrial? Absolutely not, to borrow an analogy from reporter Drew Tripp, every single domino would have to fall for this preposterous plan to work. Every single *imaginary* domino—starting with choosing the perfect twelve useful idiots among hundreds, who could be easily manipulated, too fearful to speak out against the improprieties of a court official, and a plan for ouster should a juror even look like they'd vote not guilty. This only sounds feasible for someone with an award-winning script writing team at the helm. My mouth was agape throughout the entire sham of a press conference. The more they talked, the more I wondered if Dick, Jim, and I had spent six weeks in the same courtroom at the same trial. What in the world were they even talking about? What did I—we—do wrong? I know what happened in the jury room during deliberations. We were true to our oath. After considerable thought, I decided to approach the defense's baseless allegations by discussing only the things for which I have firsthand knowledge. I will do this across three areas: the press conference, the formal motion, and a nationally televised interview.

Point Made During the Press Conference	Comment for Further Clarity
"Some jurors would not talk to us… we had lots of doors slammed in our face while looking for folks that would talk to us."	My phone never rang, and no one ever came to my house, as was the case with several other jurors.
"Alex thanked us for spending our weekends on the dirt roads of Colleton County. We're city boys and have seen places we didn't believe existed in this state."	Excuse me, mister(s)? This is gross, and not unlike the gun comment you made in opening "you people have a lot of guns; we don't in downtown Columbia." The subtext of these statements are myopic and disgusting. It sounds like they honestly expected to hear banjo music while conducting their "shoe-leather" investigation.
"There would be no smoke breaks. Dick acted like the juror's rights were violated and intimidated this was wrong."	I don't recall hearing this. However, six is ½ of twelve. If dismissed together during deliberations, they could have continued to discuss the case outside. Secondly, it would not be fair to the others, if the process was stopped at whim for ½ of the jury. As Eric Bland said, "smoking is a privilege, not a right."

Given that stereotyping the residents of Colleton County is among the defense counsel's favorite pastimes, I'll begin with a nice southern idiom—I've got a few questions stuck in my craw. How is going to a juror's home ***unannounced***, five months after a verdict, not juror intimidation? How can such accusations be hurled when most jurors were not interviewed? Why go door-to-door on a Sunday when there is a decent probability many of us would be visiting the Lord's house? Or maybe they thought if we were not at church, we'd be huntin' or fishin' down at the crick. If the affidavits of jurors who did not deliberate were given an extraordinary amount of credence, why was no consideration given to the others we lost along the way? Afterall, some of them sat in the jury box longer than they did not. Dick, did the dust from those rural, backwoods, country dirt roads permanently stain your Mercedes?

Pause and consider the implications of all that was said on a national stage and the calculated way they used the media as their bullhorn. How did fulfilling our civic duty suddenly become part of a global scandal. We were a unified jury. We firmly adhered to Judge Newman's charge. We did not do anything wrong. Most importantly, we *were* a family who, by design, shared some very dark moments and saw things we could have lived two lifetimes without seeing because we were chosen to do so—by the very people who were now accusing us of some manufactured impropriety.

In the interest of staying in my lane, so to speak, I will now address Murdaugh's motion and the dynamic duo's *Good Morning America* interview. Team Alex peppered their motion with a considerable amount of noise which, quite frankly, served the opposite of what I believe the defense intended. For example, their incessant yammering about the fb post that was or wasn't and their game of "Will the Real Tim Stone Please Stand Up" only overshadowed the point they were trying to make. It simply plays to their preferred legal strategy designed to "confuse the listener" did not work on us, nor did it work on the majority of most sensible trial watchers. It was certainly not going to work on Judge Newman (and later Justice Toal).

Having said this, I will only speak of my interactions with Ms. Hill, and that of my fellow jurors, when applicable. I will not offer judgement on any subsequent allegations which surfaced in the wake of the press conference debacle. My main purpose is two-fold. First and foremost, I want to breakthrough the cacophony of misinformation and disinformation with a ***factual*** account of my experience and share the emotional impact Team Murdaugh's little stunt had on me. Although I suspected—and rightfully so—that it might be a bit triggering, I reread the motion carefully and chose the elements which related to my experience on the jury:

Allegation Made in Motion	Explanation for Further Clarity
Hill had frequent private conversations with the jury foreperson, a Court-appointed substitution for the foreperson the jury elected for itself, at the request of Ms. Hill.	First, the statement is layered in deception. There were not frequent private conversations. I know because all of us were together eight hours a day. It would have been obvious if one of us was frequently missing. There was nothing nefarious about the ousting of the jury elected foreperson. There was confusion on the bailiff's behalf. The haphazard phrasing makes it sound like Ms. Hill orchestrated the foreperson switcheroo.

Allegation Made in Motion	Explanation for Further Clarity
"We were pressured to reach a quick verdict… Hill told us, "This shouldn't take long."	If she said this, then why did she mention dinner would be provided? More importantly, why were we informed about how long the court was prepared for us to deliberate that night? Why were we told about sequestration plans should we need to continue into Friday or beyond.
Ms. Hill told us, after the trial, we would be famous and predicted media would request interviews.	It is common for media to want to speak with jurors after a high-profile case. Media who were interested in speaking to us gave them her card, and she passed them onto us to do with them what we chose.
Ms. Hill pressured the jury to speak as a group to reporters from a network news show.	If Ms. Hill held the amount of power, fear, and influence they are alleging she wielded over us—then don't you think the entire jury would have bent to her will when it came to speaking with the media. 1/3 of us spoke to various media outlets.
After the holiday, Ms. Hill came into the jury rooms more frequently	The only one who went room-to-room with the intent to manipulate was Alex Murdaugh on the night of the boat crash.

Allegation Made in Motion	Explanation for Further Clarity
Juror Affidavit: The jury frequently discussed the case during breaks before deliberations	I have said many times that we never broke our oath by talking about the case to others OR one another. We did speak to each other until around 3:50 pm on March 2, 2023—when deliberations began.
Juror Affidavit: I had questions about his guilt but voted guilty because I felt pressured by the other jurors.	The diligence of our foreperson was discussed at length in the deliberations chapter. Likewise, our verdict was verified and validated twice in the courtroom with a chance to retract.

If nothing else, this graphic should make it abundantly clear, their motion was steeped in the commentary of numerous unreliable narrators, most of whom were frequent flyers in the spin room and all of whom had some sort of hidden agenda. A raging tempest was about to engulf Colleton County and Alex's jury was holding on for dear life. We, the jury, were flung into the machinations of a madman with zero regard for anybody but himself and his team of enablers. While I appreciated the moral support, one thing I heard a few too many times after the press conference was, "If you have nothing to hide; then you have nothing to fear." First, it is never a good idea to say this to anyone who is at the center of someone else's scheme, especially when it is being spearheaded by a group who has successfully gamed the system for decades. Now here we were, the jury that Alex Murdaugh handpicked was being put on trial for delivering our unanimous, true and just verdict based on the evidence.

Once the adrenaline rush turned to intermittent bursts of angst, I turned my focus away from the preposterous allegations and tried to understand and process why. It was clearly a flex move because Murdaugh World did not get the verdict they wanted. The morning after the presser, Dick and Jim turned *Good Morning America* into a de facto bully pulpit. They threatened the entire jury live, via satellite, from our state capital and did not mince words when they put us on notice, effectively leaving the twelve of us rattled:

Talking Point from their *GMA* Interview	My Reaction
"From what a juror told us, a lot of these folks just don't want to get involved, but they're going to be involved. If we get a hearing every one of them is going to have to testify in an open court as to what happened and what didn't happen."	To hear this broadcast on national television was frightening. This is turning the table and putting us on trial for something that had absolutely nothing to do with us.

Talking Point from their *GMA* Interview	My Reaction
"I'm concerned these jurors don't understand the import of what's getting ready to happen."	Dick, Jim: we saw through all your smoke screens. We listened to every word you said, and we know gibberish when we hear it. We are not country bumpkins afraid to question "authority." And yes, we understood full well, what was about to happen.
"They need to get lawyers. They need to understand they may have some exposure, and they need to be careful before they start talking to the FBI, SLED, or even us."	I have made myself clear on how deeply Dick and Jim's words resonated with me. Eric Bland summed it up best calling their remarks "offensive" and "threatening" to the jurors.
"We are reasonably informed on a group text last week, when these allegations began to surface, one of the jurors said, "who's talking?"	First and foremost, there was nothing malicious about our group chat. We became very close and wanted to stay in touch. Plus, our chat started after the verdict when we were officially dismissed from service. This is a common practice among jurors who have spent countless hours together week-after-week, especially in such an emotionally charged case. The context of the question was who is spreading lies?

Talking Point from their *GMA* Interview	My Reaction
"We are going to subpoena witnesses, jurors, and other individuals to court and subpoena phone records and emails."	I had absolutely nothing to hide. But it is excessive to have access to all our e-mails, texts, etc. It is an invasion of privacy and serves no purpose.
"I met with Alec in person and showed him the affidavits. He's been a lawyer for a long time. He was shaking, and he was shocked."	They expected the court of public opinion to believe that Mr. rig-a-jury appeared distressed over these manufactured allegations. Give me a break.

Since we did not fall into line with an acquittal, they were upping the game and coming after each one of us. I can only describe the shock I endured in the days following that press conference to an image familiar to most everyone. It felt like I was strolling along the sidewalk happily whistling a little ditty, when a piano suddenly fell from stories above only to flatten me. I had no idea what to do or what to expect, but what I did know, was that I—we, the jury—did absolutely nothing wrong. Concern weighted on me in the days following those bombshell allegations, while #TeamBlameSomeoneAnyone were proving to be their own best hype squad, talking to anyone who would listen. It escalated quickly and became much worse than anything I could have ever imagined and much bigger than anything I'd ever experienced. This gambit was fraught with so much uncertainty, but there was one thing I was certain of—I needed a lawyer.

CHAPTER 3:
TALK TO MY LAWYER

The presser Dick and Jim held before the South Carolina Court of Appeals marked the official kickoff of their intimidation campaign, which, spoiler alert, would galvanize the total ruination of an elected official's personal and professional reputation, while also enshrouding our unanimous verdict in doubt and uncertainty.

Alex's defense team remained true to the Murdaugh brand. It does not matter if the exposure is good or if it's bad, just stay in the news! And boy did they. The allegations of jury tampering were inescapable. It was all over social media, cable news, YouTube channels, and streaming services. As if the initial stress of what they were purporting was not enough, seeing those chaos Muppets at every turn was not helpful in the least. In addition, my phone was blowing up for at least a week with media seeking interviews. I was not talking to anyone; I was barely comfortable having a phone conversation about this with my friends and family.

As mentioned earlier, we were actively working on the book when this came to pass, and knowing how much they enjoy turning the benign into the controversial, Shana and I ceased talking business via text and email. With abiding faith and unwavering integrity, I was confident the truth would prevail, but how did that compare to Team Murdaugh's money, clout, and power? To them we were just a pack of simpletons who lived out in the sticks protecting our gun arsenals. In their eyes, we were exceedingly susceptible to the power of suggestion and incapable of thinking critically about the evidence.

After the presser on Tuesday, followed by the *Good Morning America* interview on Wednesday, it did not take long for the good guys, donning their white hats, to recognize we were at a disadvantage when it came to Murdaugh World. Without hesitation, Eric Bland and Ronnie Richter pointed their steeds toward the dusty dirt roads of Colleton County. The day after Dick and Jim's *Good Morning America* appearance, Eric Bland posted the following announcement on X (formerly Twitter):

At the press conference earlier this week, Dick Harpootlian suggested that the jurors should get lawyers. How offensive is that? How threatening is that? If any juror feels like they need legal representation or just to get some advice, please feel free to call Ronnie Richter and me. We would not charge a fee for the consultation or representation. It's just disgraceful the people are having to pay for legal fees in this most unfortunate situation.

One of my fellow jurors let me know she retained Eric, and I quickly did the same. Just talking to Ronnie Richter and Eric Bland unburdened me, and I knew we were in excellent hands. No matter the situation, it is often intimidating to speak with law enforcement. It was a relief when Eric said he would be present for our individual interviews with SLED agents.

Once each of us talked to investigators and finalized our sworn affidavits, the wheels of justice felt like they came to a grinding halt. One week there'd be a tsunami of updates, then we'd hear nothing. I just wanted this over, and I am quite certain many, if not all, of my fellow jurors shared this sentiment. In true Dick and Jim fashion, when new filings became available, controversy was not far behind.

One of the first calculated "defense strategies," a term I use loosely, was the Fox Nation release *Fall of the House of Murdaugh* (a Dick and Jim production). This docuseries was not slated for release until around mid-September. There is nothing coincidental about it suddenly becoming available weeks earlier than planned on August 31 (2023), to be exact. This happened to be Labor Day weekend, and the same day Jim would rage on *Cuomo*, signaling there are jury-related concerns pertaining to Alex's double murder trial. The series also happened to drop over the holiday weekend, giving viewers plenty of time to binge. *Fall of the House of Murdaugh* showed the Alex they desperately tried to depict at trial, while simultaneously creating a fantasy world where once again, he was the victim of a botched investigation, a rush to judgement, and ultimately a jury that got it wrong. Because in Alex's words, "the jury did not have a feel for how many lies went into this story." To which I would like to say, "We know how many lies went into your story, Alex. In fact, there were so many, we lost count." It provided some notable insight into this never-ending story of wealth, power, and greed. However, there was an overt agenda, yet that was not what I found troubling. The utter hypocrisy and disregard for everyone except Alex Murdaugh was quite frankly just plain gross. For example, anytime Dick and Jim have a stage and a captive audience, be it a televised interview, press conference, or the courtroom floor, they complain ceaselessly about the case's widespread coverage, as well as its pervasiveness within the true crime community. They disparage authors, podcasters, and producers all while admonishing devotees of the genre. The duo—Dick especially—have even taken brutal swipes at some of their colleagues who never hesitate to speak truth to power when their expertise is needed.

While watching *Fall of the House of Murdaugh* it seemed obvious to me that this series was always part of the plan for the defense counsel. I, for one, have never, ever watched a true crime docuseries where there is live footage of a legal team strategizing and preparing for the next day's direct or cross-examination. Likewise, Alex's penchant for breaking rules, coupled with Jim's tendency to bend policies added a skosh of scandal to the show's launch which gave it extra publicity. Jim recorded Alex reading from a "journal he kept during the trial" for producers of the Fox Nation series. This is a violation of SCDC policy which states, "South Carolina inmates are not allowed to give media interviews. We believe that victims of crime should not have to see or hear the person who victimized them or their family member on the news." Both Jim Griffin and Alex Murdaugh are veteran lawyers in South Carolina. They know the rules, and they chose to break them. Nearly a year later, this still disgusts me. It goes way beyond the male privilege which is engrained in those three. I am appalled for their flagrant disregard of the victims—especially Maggie's family. The only thing that mattered was having new and exclusive footage for their pet project. There were in-house or rather "in-big-house" consequences for Alex, and Jim got a warning letter from SCDC.

After the docuseries premiere and the press conference, Murdaugh World was suspiciously quiet which always offered pause for concern. We had no idea what was happening next, when, or if, there would be a hearing. Then boom—Dick and Jim came in like a wrecking ball with a writ of prohibition asking the Supreme Court of South Carolina remove Judge Newman from presiding over all future Murdaugh matters. They planted this seed in September suggesting he would likely be called as a witness during a future hearing about the jury tampering allegations. It further laid claim that "Newman had made numerous statements in and out of court expressing his personal opinion about Murdaugh's guilt, legal issues and trial strategy." I was enraged they would stoop as low as to question the integrity of Judge Newman. I felt gutted for him, as this was happening when his tenure was about to come to an end. His impeccable reputation, celebrated career, and commitment to justice meant nothing in their quest for a new trial.

On a personal note, this gave me concern for who would be called to replace him. Please understand this worry was unrelated to Alex and/or his defense counsel. It had everything to do with us. One minute we were ordinary citizens who completed our jury service, then suddenly we were at the center of an investigation and our verdict was under scrutiny. And no matter the outcome, this would be a watershed moment—for better or worse—impacting both the jury and judicial systems. Now we would have to do this without the person who prioritized our safety, comfort and anonymity. I am not implying we did not have absolute faith in whomever Chief Justice (Ret.) Beatty would choose as a replacement. It was just difficult to imagine how this might all play out without Judge Newman's stern, level-headedness. In late December, we learned of former Chief Justice (Ret.) Jean Toal's appointment in this brief order:

With the Honorable Clifton Newman presiding, the Defendant was convicted of the murders of Margaret Kennedy Branstetter Murdaugh and Paul Terry Murdaugh on March 2, 2023, and sentenced on March 3, 2023. On October 27, 2023, the Defendant filed a motion for a new trial. I find that Judge Clifton Newman has requested to be removed from all post-trial matters related to the above-referenced matters. IT IS HEREBY ORDERED that the Honorable Jean Hoefer Toal, retired Chief Justice of the Supreme Court of South Carolina, be assigned exclusive jurisdiction for the limited purpose of presiding over Defendant's motion for a new trial in the above matters. Justice Toal shall decide all matters pertaining to these cases, including motions to appoint and relieve counsel, and shall retain jurisdiction over these cases regardless of where she may be assigned to hold court and may schedule such hearings as may be necessary at any time without regard as to whether there is a term of court scheduled.

This change of guard reminded me of a crucial life lesson I temporarily forgot—don't get bogged down in the opinions and experiences of others. Justice Beatty appointed Judge Newman; he knew who would best fill the enormous shoes Judge Newman left behind. I went down a few Google and social media rabbit holes and when that was not enough, I asked a few people who had direct knowledge of the revered jurist. Afterall, she was selected to come out of retirement to preside over this storyline arc of *As Murdaugh World Turns*. Media reports of Beatty's selection indicated there was a definite chasm between former colleagues of Justice Toal, suspicious trial watchers, and an opportunistic independent news source:

Charlie Condon (Former AG South Carolina): Former Chief Justice Jean Toal is the perfect choice to preside over Alex Murdaugh's motion for a new trial. She is smart, well versed in the law, and fair.

Jay Bender (Columbia Attorney): I can't imagine anybody better suited than Toal." I think she will recognize and appreciate its significance to the judicial system of South Carolina. She's smart, thorough, she'll come prepared, she will be better prepared than the lawyers. She will ask insightful questions and she will make a ruling and she'll do it with dispatch.

Dayne Phillips (Lawyer at Price Benowitz): It will come down to a credibility determination by former Chief Justice Toal, and that is going to be something that the whole world will be watching very closely; to have her she is an absolute giant in the legal community. Her experience and reputation are beyond reproach.

I detest the drama that often dominates social media. However, I fell straight through the looking glass reading posts immersed in conspiracy and doubt. There were stories of Justice Toal's lengthy friendship with Dick Harpootlian running counter to a genuine tweet by Creighton Waters when seeing her at an event—long before her appointment to the Murdaugh case. The internet was left confused wondering if she was conflicted. Some speculation and doubt about Justice Toal included comments such as:

@tigerdale: I can't help but feel this is about to go in the wrong direction

@biggerlouder: With all the sneaky, behind closed doors corruption in this state. I'd like to know how this justice leaned in cases, and who, if anyone, she is beholden too. At this point I trust no one.

@Beverly Harvey: This is heartbreaking. It feels like the bad guys win.

@Greatpyrsrg: The fix is in

@CandJ_GOP: SC remains a fraudulent wasteland of injustice

In addition, some once dependable news sources became about as reliable as the *National Enquirer*. Pushing salacious and distorted headlines, ignoring the ***facts***, and revising the ***truth*** became their new business model. Ethics were seemingly cast aside to be the first news outlet to break a story. It is a bit ironic, too, that the defense leaked like a sieve to one publication, who ended up doing very little to advance their cause in the court of public opinion. Reading this nonsense left me with more questions than answers; after realizing this was an exercise in futility, I turned my worries over to the Lord and trusted Justice Toal was the person Maggie, Paul, and the jury needed in this moment.

CHAPTER 4:
I'M GONNA WASH THAT
MAN RIGHT OUTTA MY HAIR

After Justice Jean Toal's appointment in late December (2023), we finally had some indication the new year would bring resolve to this Murdaugh madness—or at least the part that affected us—the jury of his peers. In no more than three days of her appointment, the public learned she held a teleconference with both legal teams.

Reports indicated our anonymity would remain protected during the public and televised proceedings scheduled for January. For this, I was grateful. Many of my fellow jurors were already uneasy about having to testify, which was only exacerbated by the case's reawakened intrigue and nonstop press coverage. They coveted their anonymity now more than ever. Secondly, I strongly agree public transparency was nonnegotiable. Judge Ito (of OJ fame) said, "If you take the cameras out of the courtroom, then you hide, I think, a certain measure of truth from the public. And it's very important for the American public to know"; particularly since the Murdaugh tentacles extended far beyond the courthouses of the Fourteenth Judicial Circuit. For Team Murdaugh, the only thing that has stood between them and a game of "Phone-a-fix" is a poor connection. The Lowcountry deserved to see the justice system at work, especially since this was the first time in Alex Murdaugh's entire life that he was being held to account for his actions.

Alex, Dick, and Jim, the poster children for privilege, mistakenly thought they could control every element of that evidentiary hearing, but Justice Toal was not having any part of that. They may have given Lady Justice two black eyes during their last head-to-head, but this time she'd not go down without a fight.

As mentioned previously, public opinion was divided about her appointment to the case. Some of the most balanced and dependable voices expressed skepticism. I had to satisfy my curiosity about the Justice who was tasked with resolving this nightmare. First and foremost, I removed myself from the social media bluster to learn a little about Justice Toal and her time on the Supreme Court. I felt this would be the best way to offer an informed opinion about my experience in her courtroom. Her career has been nothing short of incredible. Justice Toal's decades of hard work and her commitment to justice has earned her a prominent place in the annals of our judicial system. South Carolina Courts notes a few of her accomplishments:

> Chief Justice Jean Hoefer Toal began her service as an Associate Justice on the Supreme Court of South Carolina on March 17, 1988, becoming the first woman to serve as a Justice of the South Carolina Supreme Court. When she was admitted to the bar in 1968, women comprised less than one percent of the licensed lawyers in South Carolina. Now almost 20 percent of South Carolina's lawyers are women. Justice Toal consulted with Ruth Bader Ginsburg, when she was a Columbia University law professor and a consultant for the Women's Rights Project at the ACLU. They worked on strategy and briefs, which Ginsburg stated, 'addressed novel constitutional issues related to the analysis of sexually discriminatory classifications under the Constitution and were part of a nationwide push to achieve full equality for women under the law.'

Being a woman in a male dominated profession comes with its own unique set of rules and difficulties. Combining that with the chauvinistic and misogynistic tendencies of Murdaugh World might sound intimidating or discouraging to some women, but Justice Toal proved well prepared for any of their courtroom shenanigans. This understanding helped keep my imagination from totally running wild.

Maya Angelou said, "When someone shows you who they are, believe them the first time." This has spoken deeply to me, but

I don't always excel at following her sage advice. However, when Justice Toal showed me—and the world—who she was, I had no problem trusting that she ruled her courtroom with an iron gavel. I was certain, if she ever chose to preside over a television courtroom, Judge Judy just might find herself out of a job. Dick and Jim certainly pushed the ever-patient Judge Newman to the point of reprimand, but his gentle nature often disguised the scolding. Justice Toal, however, was neither reserved nor subtle "Toal reprimanded Harpootlian, a longtime lawyer, for his continued suggestion that Hill sought to enrich herself by pushing jurors toward a guilty verdict. She harshly quipped, 'I hope that's the last time you're gonna repeat that until I ask for that again; Let's move on.'" Clearly, she was not there to play, which made the two weeks leading up to the evidentiary hearing a lot more tolerable. Soon we, the jury, would be reunited with one another, as well as the defendant—who we convicted of double murder just ten months prior.

My mom attended the evidentiary hearing to lend her support. Since that is about an hour and a half from Colleton County, we decided it would be best to book a hotel; especially since the hearing was slated for three days. We headed to Columbia after church and stayed in a hotel close to the courthouse. This worked out well because when we were dismissed, I would be able to go back to the room, decompress, watch the hearing, and remain far away from all news crews.

In addition to having my mom and co-author with me, my good friends, Neil and Melissa Gordon were also in town. The morning of the hearing, friends of theirs began texting around

6:30 AM saying the line was growing quickly. Mom was riding with them since SLED agents were transporting jurors to and from the courthouse. Poor Neil must have lost the coin toss, as he was the one who had to keep their spot in line, on that freezing, windy January morning, so the ladies could stay in the warm car. Anyone who has spent time in Columbia knows it is the hottest place in the state during the summer and the coldest in the winter. _**My**_ juror support staff and Maggie and Paul's tiny justice league of four were anxious about how the day would unfold and excited it would soon, one way or another, mark the conclusion of the lengthiest jury service known to man. Afterall, OJ's jury was only tethered for eight months.

Once all eleven jurors arrived at the courthouse, we waited for everyone to arrive before going through security. Despite the circumstances, it was wonderful to see everyone. We were genuinely excited to be reunited. In no time, we fell back into acting like the family we had become. It was so hard to believe we sat down for our first day as Alex's jury, just over one year ago.

I felt so silly thinking it would be at least two years before I ever walked into another jury room, but alas, there I sat with my fellow jurors once again. The bailiff gave us a briefing of what we could expect from the morning. Telling us, when Justice Toal was ready, we would file into the courtroom as a group, so she could address us collectively. After which we'd return to the jury room and would be called one-by-one to testify.

We lined up in the same order as we did for six weeks; however, this time we were missing our foreperson. She was given permission to testify the Friday before, due to a scheduling conflict. Being together with everyone felt pleasantly familiar, yet frustrating and unsettling. While I awaited my turn, I prayed the bad guys would not win. My faith kept me sane during all this insanity. I believed He would allow the light of truth to shine brightly through the storm that gathered each time Alex entered a courthouse. I knew God would see that we would be released from the silken fibers of Alex Murdaugh's tangled web. In turn, showing the world that our justice system has zero tolerance for ill-will and malicious half-truths.

When we took our seats in the jury box, I immediately spotted my support system in the crowded room. The room was full of trial watchers and countless media, yet there was a deadly silence, very reminiscent of the evening we delivered the verdict. Hanging heavily in the room was a fear that law enforcement's hard work, the prosecution's dedication, and our six weeks of sacrifice could be swiftly undone. Everyone in that room felt like they had a stake in the preserving of Maggie and Paul's justice and to seeing that it was not egregiously revoked except for Alex, his defense team and a couple of reporters who were eager to see the remake of SC vs. *Richard Alexander Murdaugh*. When Justice Toal took the bench, she addressed us directly, and immediately set our minds at ease:

Good morning, ladies and gentlemen of the *State vs Murdaugh* jury. I wanted to make a few opening remarks before I question each of you about the matter. You have done absolutely nothing wrong; none of you have. You didn't ask to serve but did your duty. This was an unusually difficult trial; six weeks is almost unheard of in South Carolina. It was also difficult because of the intense publicity and public interest in the case. It was difficult because of the complexity of testimony and exhibits in the case, and you acquitted yourself honorably. The question today is not about anything you did wrong; please be assured of that. I respect you, and I respect your service. I'm asking about the time you served, not about _this_ time. There has been so much drama about this matter since the verdict was rendered. My heart goes out to everyone. I thank you very much in advance for this terrible inconvenience of calling you all back together now.

Her reassurance that we had done nothing wrong was exactly what we, the jury, needed. Intellectually we knew that, but nonetheless, it was reassuring to hear that from the bench. Once she finished, we made our way back to the jury room. The individual testimony of my fellow jurors went by quickly. When each juror returned from delivering their testimony, they not only looked relieved, but also had an air of confidence and pride for safeguarding the authenticity of our unanimous verdict. Since I was the 12th juror chosen, I would take the stand last.

In the preceding weeks, I had imagined what my testimony might look like. Would I for some strange reason trip and fall into the witness stand? Would I be nervous? Would it be like one of those dreams where you open your mouth to speak, and nothing comes out? For all the ridiculous hypotheticals I ran through, I knew one thing would happen. I **_would_** look Alex Murdaugh,

Dick Harpootlian and Jim Griffin in the eye the entire time I was on the witness stand. I may not have had control over anything that happened in Murdaugh World, **_but_** they could not control **_my_** voice when I was called to speak truth to power.

I will not comment on the testimony of Juror Z, as it is not my place to do so. Should she ever choose to speak out publicly about the trial, her guilty verdict, and/or her testimony, she will do so when the time is right for her. It is not my story to tell. Days after Justice Toal's ruling, out of curiosity, I decided to watch the beginning of the hearing to see what happened while we were in the jury room. There is one moment in juror Z's testimony which I feel merits some input. As in her affidavit, she reiterated feeling pressured by her fellow jurors. The jury foreperson gave us every opportunity to continue deliberations late into the evening and into the next day (and so on). She even gave us the chance to contest our verdict before they were finalized. Lastly, Judge Newman provided two occasions in front of the defendant, his counsel, and the world to renege, and no one said a word. Return policies should never apply to a verdict, especially after ample opportunity was given to speak up.

When court resumed after the mid-morning recess, I don't think anyone knew they'd be returning to the big top, where Dick Harpootlian would put on quite a show. After lunch, Justice Toal stated, she received an e-mail from Juror Z's attorney wanting to "enhance" her earlier testimony and clarify some things about her initial affidavit (from August of 2023). Justice Toal, with Creighton Waters in agreement, denied giving her "another bite at the apple, because witnesses can't get back on the stand and then try to come back later and close the loop of inconsistencies." Dick desperately wanted to go head-to-head with the revered justice, claiming the way she questioned jurors was flawed. Further stating, "And there's no reason we should not be able to ask her further questions." When I heard that, I had no words. Dick's courtroom moxie is so astounding, it's like someone puts me on mute and renders me speechless.

Secondly, at the status conference held two weeks prior to the hearing, Justice Toal laid down clear parameters to avoid "a wholesale exploration of the clerk's conduct." This involved putting limitations on who could and could not be called to testify. Witnesses she scratched off the defense's list included: state prosecutor Creighton Waters, Judge Clifton Newman, the one remaining alternate, and Juror 785. However, after Ms. Hill's testimony, Justice Toal was left with serious questions about her reliability and allowed Rhonda McElveen, Barnwell Clerk of Court and the one remaining alternate (Juror 741) to testify. To me, it felt like McElveen's testimony did more to advance the prosecution's claims than to impeach the former Colleton County clerk, among the most noteworthy points in her testimony are listed below:

- Creighton Waters asked if it's not unusual for court staff to have private conversations about the events of the day, without the jury being present, which McElveen agrees with. She said she doesn't know of Hill having any improper conversations with jurors.

- She never heard or was told that Hill was having conversations with jurors about the defendant's guilt or innocence. And continued that she would have without a doubt gone to Judge Newman had she seen or heard anything untoward about Hill communicating with jurors.

- She never once saw anything during the trial that caused her to go to Judge Newman.

Clerk McElveen was a very credible witness, and I had absolutely no doubt she was telling the truth. It was evident, in my opinion, that Dick took the vast majority of what she said out of context and spun it into something more sinister.

For his final stunt, Dick offered Justice Toal one final opportunity to hear from Juror 785 because she was "just across the street." Justice Toal, however, was not interested. The only arrow left in Harpootlian's quiver, was Juror 741, who completed an affidavit at Dick's office earlier that same day. Juror 741 was the one remaining alternate who, per Dick's request, remained at the courthouse while we were in deliberations. When Meadors cross examined her, he focused on highlighting the discrepancies between her proxy affidavit via Holli Miller (Dick's paralegal) last summer with the one she completed on the day of the evidentiary hearing.

We were all wondering how long it would take Justice Toal to make her ruling. Would an announcement be made tomorrow, a few days or even next week? I think every trial watcher, both in and out of the courtroom, was surprised she called a brief recess and announced she would return with her ruling. I never knew same day service was a thing in government—especially in the justice system.

The opposing punditry was maddening. Getting myself all spun up in commentary, was not helpful. So, I turned down the television's volume, tuned out Court TV, then tuned into myself while I sat prayerfully in silence. At the end of the day, Justice Toal's opinion was truly all that mattered. Upon seeing her enter the courtroom and take a seat, I had a pit in my stomach and lump in my throat. I gave the television a little volume, and, like so many times before, I turned it over to God.

I felt such a sense of relief once Justice Toal officially denied Richard Alexander Murdaugh a new trial. Overturning this verdict would have been an incredible injustice to Maggie and Paul; it would have resulted in the revictimization of their families, not to mention the irrevocable damage it would do to the newly reborn Fourteenth Judicial Circuit of South Carolina. The world was apparently as nervous about the outcome of this hearing as everyone in the courtroom. They were not shy about celebrating Justice Toal's findings and immediately shared their joy on social media:

@Cornerstoner: Thaaaaank You, Judge! (no gavel emoji.... so u get a hammer....a hammer of JUSTICE!)

@judywhiting1675: He's a CONVICTED MURDER-ER....go back to jail...do NOT pass go

@richardberriman: Lock him up! Oh right.... never mind

@melodyemeyers370: THANK YOU LORD!! HE IS WHERE HE BELONGS....FOREVER AND EVER AND A DAY!

@Vbluevital: Good news, no new trial.

Beyond any shred of reasonable doubt, we, the jury, knew what the evidence showed. The evidence—and the evidence alone—led to our unanimous and true verdict. My heart and head always knew God would not allow someone who committed "the most heinous crime known to man" another chance to prove his "innocence" and potentially walk free. We are taught from an early age that good triumphs over evil. During that year long journey, it seemed as if *SC* vs *Richard Alexander Murdaugh* might be the exception. When this doubt crept in, I'd cling that much tighter to my deep, enduring faith as a source of light on even the darkest of days, for the immortal words of Dr. Martin Luther King, Jr. reminds us, "We shall overcome because the arc of the moral universe is long, but it bends toward justice.

EPILOGUE:
NO REST FOR THE WICKED

Eric "EB" Bland, Attorney
September 2024

After the double murder conviction in March 2023 for the killing of Maggie and Paul, the lights never went dim. Even still through today, the Murdaugh circus remains a constant. Following his murder conviction, Team Murdaugh filed a motion seeking relief from the Confessed Judgment that Alex gave to the Satterfield estate in May 2022 in the amount of $4,305,000.00. This was the full amount of both settlements that were obtained for the February 2018 death of Gloria Satterfield from Nautilus and Lloyds of London then misappropriated by Cory Fleming and Alex Murdaugh. The Satterfield sons got no money from this large settlement. Team Murdaugh tried to argue that Alex should be relieved from the $4,305,000.00 Confessed Judgment that he voluntarily gave the Satterfield estate because they were able to recover in excess of $9,300,000 from sources other than Murdaugh. These funds were obtained through settlements with banks, law firms, Chad Westerndorf and Cory Fleming. They were essentially arguing the Satterfields had recovered enough money, and Alex should get the benefit of the payments made by others. Fortunately, in August 2023, Circuit Court Judge Bentley Price denied Murdaugh's motion, and the judgment against him is good for ten years from the date of its entry. Murdaugh tried to appeal this ruling but ultimately it was dismissed on appeal.

Next Murdaugh tried to add the Satterfields as third-party defendants in the Federal Court Action brought by Nautilus Insurance Company to recover the approximately 3.8 million dollars he misappropriated from the May 2019 Gloria Satterfield settlement. Fortunately, Federal Court Judge Richard Gergel also denied Murdaugh's motion to add the Satterfields to that action, and they were spared of being further victimized by him.

The 2021 Labor Day roadside shooting charges against Alex and Cousin Eddie remain pending. In August 2023 Team Murdaugh held a much-heralded press conference in front of the South Carolina Court of Appeals where Alex's lawyers boldly proclaimed that former Colleton County Clerk of Court Becky Hill had allegedly made inappropriate comments to the sitting jurors (all of the jurors even the alternates) about Alex's guilt and the inferences which should be drawn from his testimony. They said she influenced many of the jurors into voting Alex guilty of the murders. Harpootlian said the jurors were going to have to lawyer up because he had talked to most of them. And he allegedly got confirmation of Ms. Hill's comments going beyond normal ministerial communications and touched on the substance of the case. Harpootlian claimed Murdaugh would get a new trial and that a travesty of justice had been committed. I was outraged by these statements.

First, the entire jury was polled after the verdict, and all of the jurors proclaimed and confirmed, with their hands raised to Judge Newman's questions that their verdicts were of their own free will; they were not coerced or the product of pressure from anyone or the other jurors. Their verdict was from their own conscience after hearing the testimony, receiving the evidence, and listening to Judge Newman's jury instructions. Harpootlian said he was going to file a motion for a new trial based on the allegations against Ms. Hill and the improper removal of the "egg lady" juror by Judge Newman.

Harpootlian then argued Judge Newman should not hear this motion for a new trial. Judge Newman was scheduled to retire by December 31, 2023, under state law because he was 72 years old. Harpootlian argued Judge Newman was conflicted from hearing the motion for a new trial because he had given television interviews, spoke about the trial his alma mater, Cleveland State University. and because of the very personal and pointed statements he made when he sentenced Alex Murdaugh to a double life sentence the day after the double murder convictions.

In September 2023, Alex Murdaugh pleaded guilty in front of Federal Judge Richard Gergel, to approximately 24 charges of financial crimes for many of his former clients/victims, many of whom he said he loved and considered friends. He said he wanted to do right by them. The sentencing was to happen after a pre-sentence report was done by the Federal Justice Department.

In October 2023, Judge Newman scheduled the criminal trial of the Satterfield charges for the financial theft to occur after Thanksgiving in November 2023. Harpootlian immediately filed a motion for continuance and said he was to be out of the country for Thanksgiving with his wife Jamie, who is an ambassador in Slovenia. To Harpootlian's anger, Judge Newman denied the motion. Thereafter, Team Murdaugh made a motion before the South Carolina Supreme Court to have Judge Newman removed from hearing the Satterfield criminal trial, arguing he was conflicted and could not act fairly when presiding over the trial. It was decided that Judge Newman would, indeed, preside over the Satterfield criminal trial, and it would go forward, as scheduled, on Monday November 27, 2024.

On the day of the trial when jury selection was to occur, Team Murdaugh announced they had reached an agreement with the South Carolina Assistant Attorney General Creighton Waters that Alex would plead guilty to more than twenty state felony crimes, with a recommended and agreed sentence of 27 years in state prison. If Judge Newman agreed to the sentence, Alex Murdaugh would not be parole eligible until he completed a minimum of at least 23 years of the 27-year sentence. Alex was approximately 55 years old at the time, so on that sentence alone, he would most likely spend the rest of his natural life in a state maximum security prison for the crimes to which he pled guilty. Even though he will be given credit for being incarcerated continuously since October 2021, Alex will be well into his seventies before he is eligible for release. Since the life span for those who live in a maximum-security prison is thought to be much less than the regular life span of men, Alex most likely will not make it to the conclusion of his state financial crime sentence.

At the plea hearing, many of Alex's victims spoke out against him including Tony Satterfield, Ginger Hadwin (Gloria's sister), Jordan Jinks, Pamela Pickney. Attorneys Justin Bamburg, Mark Tinsley, and I spoke on behalf of our clients. After we all spoke, Alex chose to speak for more than 45 minutes, where his hubris and narcissism shown brightly as he tried to justify why he committed these heinous crimes. And used this opportunity to, once again, proclaim his innocence in the murders of Maggie and Paul. Judge Newman gave a chilling explanation of the sentence he **_was_** to impose, and then sentenced Alex to 27 years.

After Judge Newman's recusal, it was decided that former Chief Justice of the South Carolina Supreme Court Jean Toal, who was on senior circuit court judge status, would schedule and hear the pending motion for a new trial. At the end of January 2024, Justice Toal scheduled and heard the pending motion for a new trial in the double murder cases. The hearing was internationally televised. Justice Toal heard from all the twelve seated jurors who voted on Alex's guilt and one of the alternate jurors. After hearing the testimony of the witnesses, including former clerk of court Becky Hill, Justice Toal denied Murdaugh's motion for a new trial. While she declared that she found some of Becky Hill's testimony not to be credible, she conclusively found that the jury's verdicts were not influenced by anything that Becky Hill may have said or done and that no one was pressured into their verdicts. She held that the fact that all the jurors were individually polled after they rendered their verdicts and declared that the verdict was of their own free will was persuasive.

Justice Toal said it is a dangerous precedent to permit jurors, months after a trial, who may be subject to direct and indirect pressure to start questioning their verdicts. The system needs finality. Of course, Alex has appealed Justice Toal's decision and has argued that she incorrectly applied the South Carolina standard for jury interference instead of the federal standard from the Remmer case as pronounced by the United States Supreme Court.

This comes as no surprise that Alex would appeal this ruling. Alex has also appealed his murder convictions from the trial based on several issues, including but not limited to, failure to grant a change of venue for the trial and evidentiary rulings made by Judge Newman regarding the admission of his financial crimes as an explanation of the motive for the murders. Again, no surprise. All convicted felons usually appeal. What is unusual is the South Carolina Supreme Court as of the date of the publishing of this book, agreed to accept the appeal on the denial of a motion for a new trial directly without the appeal being heard first by the intermediate court of appeals. The South Carolina Supreme Court has not scheduled oral arguments yet on the appeal.

In April 2024, Alex Murdaugh was sentenced to 40 years by Federal Judge Richard Gergel in connection with the September 2023 plea of guilt by Alex as to the federal financial crimes. Judge Gergel had given notice that he would consider giving an upward enhanced sentence beyond the recommended sentence of 20-25 years. Alex stood before Judge Gergel and admitted his crimes, told the judge he was willing to accept the sentence, and his lawyer Jim Griffin did not object to Judge Gergel considering the additional enhancement. Judge Gergel excoriated Alex when he sentenced him to 40 years. He said that his crimes were different than Madoff's and Sam Bankmen Fried's victims. He said those victims were trying to make money on the money they invested. Instead, the Murdaugh victims needed the money that Alex stole from them because they lost loved ones who were income earners, or the client was permanently disabled and needed the money for medical bills or to care for their families. As usual, after the sentence was pronounced, Alex appealed the sentence to the Federal Fourth Circuit Court of Appeals and argued that by sentencing him to 40 years constituted a violation of Alex's 8th amendment rights and that the sentence was cruel and unusual punishment. The appeal has not been scheduled for oral arguments as of the publishing of this book. What is interesting is that Dick Harpootlian did not show up for Alex's sentencing by Judge Gergel, nor did he sign on to the appellate brief filed by attorney Jim Griffin on behalf of Alex Murdaugh.

On January 1, 2024, Judge Newman retired as a circuit court judge, and Becky Hill resigned her position as Colleton County Clerk of Court on March 25, 2024. She is currently under criminal investigation for alleged abuses while she was in office. Her son was investigated and charged for allegedly committing wiretap violations in the summer of 2023. Dick Harpootlian lost his re-election bid for his senate seat when he lost his primary race to current house member Russell Ott. Harpootlian did not see this happening. He was shocked. There are anecdotal stories of voters who voted against him after previously voting for him because of some of the statements and actions he had taken on behalf of Alex Murdaugh during the previous four years. It turns out that Harpootlian bet on the wrong horse and may have found himself on the wrong side of history.

Alex is currently serving his time in a maximum-security prison in protective custody. Rumors have circulated that Alex is enjoying his time and making friends in the prison where he is housed. There are rumors that he is participating in illegal gaming operations and providing legal advice to his fellow inmates. Early on in his sentence, he lost his phone privileges because of a multitude of prison violations, which is just par for the course. Buster Murdaugh gave his one and only television interview to Fox News in September 2023 where he explained that he had nothing to do with the death of Stephen Smith which occurred in July 2015 and that he continued to believe in his father's innocence for the killing of his mother and brother. Since the interview, Buster has filed a defamation civil lawsuit and a detailed complaint against many media companies who did documentaries and a journalist who he said defamed him by linking him as being a part of Stephen Smith's death and suggesting that he had a relationship with Stephen. This case is in its infancy stages and will be interesting to watch unfold. Buster certainly has the right to protect and sue over his reputation being wrongfully defamed. The defendants will argue that truth is a defense to the allegations and that Buster is a public figure or a quasi-public figure and cannot show that the defendants acted with actual malice (*New York Times v. Sullivan*).

In conclusion, the fall-out from Alex's litany of crimes and the lives that he has broken continues to be felt today. He tarnished the reputation of Hampton County, as well as the state of South Carolina. In the eyes of the citizens of South Carolina and the world, he has caused significant and maybe permanent damage to the state's legal bar.

AFTERWORD:
MURDER WAS THE CASE

By: Gigi McKelvey

We all accept jury duty as our civic duty to the communities we call home. It is our way to keep our little corners of the world safe from people who shouldn't be among us. It is also our way to be sure potentially innocent people aren't wrongly convicted for crimes they didn't commit. Juries are the heartbeat of the judicial system. Prosecutors and defense attorneys devote weeks, months, and sometimes years to their respective cases only to leave all of their hard work in the hands of twelve strangers. At the end of the day, nothing else matters other than the decision of a jury of the defendant's peers.

We don't often think of the toll that being on a jury has for the members long after the verdict is handed down. We pluck average citizens from their comfortable daily lives and expose them to some of the most horrific images and videos they will ever see in their lifetime. The toll is great for many. Even on the most graphic days of this trial, the jurors in this case were focused on the task at hand, weighing the evidence and coming to a fair and just verdict.

Amie Williams stood out to me from the first day of jury selection. She was always focused and was the hardest juror on the panel to read. Her dedication to justice for the victims, Paul and Maggie Murdaugh, was evident from day one.

As a South Carolinian, I am grateful to Amie and all of the jurors who sacrificed for weeks to bring resolution to this case, restoring faith in their community and also to our entire state, that justice will be served no matter who stands accused. This was one of the biggest cases the state of South Carolina has ever seen and in spite of a packed courtroom full of media and a front lawn overflowing with bright lights and cameras, they focused on their job.

They handled this case with the utmost care and we all knew this case was in good hands long before deliberations began. Thank you for your service, Amie. You, along with your fellow jurors, are a classic example of how a jury should work - together in the name of justice.

ACKNOWLEDGEMENTS

There are a host of people to whom we need to extend our collective appreciation. Thank you to Neil and Melissa Gordon for being on this journey with us from the very beginning and cheering us on every step of the way. This long road would have been full of potholes if not for your guidance. We owe a huge debt of gratitude to our editor, Elizabeth Dardes, our beta reader Kim Poovey, and Renaissance woman, Melissa Minkser. Thank you to trial superstar Dr. Kenny Kinsey for writing the Foreword, Legal Eagle Eric Bland for the epilogue, and *Law and Crime* correspondent Gigi McKelvey for writing the Afterword. Thank you to Ashley Holland who brought an image of Lady Justice to life for our signature plates.

I am eternally grateful Amie Williams trusted me to write her story. I would like to extend my deepest appreciation to the reporters/authors who were beyond kind and always willing to answer my most random of questions and/or point me in the right direction: Valerie Bauerlein, Michael Dewitt, and Jason Ryan—Thank you. Thank you to my favorite podcasters whose hard work helped me immeasurably and whose enthusiasm for our project kept me writing: Kassidy O'Connell (*Legal Updates with Kassidy*), Paul (*Reporting Live From my Sofa*), Lauren and Dr. John Mathias (*Hidden True Crime*), Kathy (*Gossip, Rumor, and Innuendo*), Joel Waldman and the COE (*Surviving the Survivor*), Emily (*Emily D. Baker)*, and, of course, Gigi McKelvey (*Pretty Lies and Alibis*). Thanks to my crew— Annie, Amy, Ben and Grayson—at *10 to Life* and *Seriously* for the emails of encouragement and overall excitement for our project.

I also want to express an individual note of thanks to Elizabeth Dardes and Kim Poovey for your hard work and endless supply of kind words about our project. Your confidence and belief in my writing and voice was the reassurance I needed to "just keep swimming" to the finish line. Marsha Vinoski, thanks for sharing your love of true crime and words with me so many moons ago and for always being my human thesaurus.

And to my wonderful friends who let me ramble about Alex Murdaugh endlessly for nearly two years. Thank you for not taking my absence personally and supporting me through it all. As always, thank you, Latesha Smith, for saving me from myself when I melted down over the citation page. A big thank you to Mindy Lucas for lending your talent to create our book trailer and reels. I am also grateful that Joeseph Ortiz kept me supplied with caffeine and stuck around through the chaos.

Thanks Baby G. for letting Mommy chase this dream— more walks, games of fetch, and beach days are coming soon— right after I take a Rip Van Winkle sized nap. Last but never ever least, MB, you've always believed this could become a reality, and here we are.

— Shana Hirsch

END NOTES

Preface

p. xii Chapter title inspired by Chuck Berry's "Have Mercy Judge."

p. xii Statistics: Chalabi, Mona. "What Are the Chances of Serving on A Jury?" *FiveThirtyEight. ABCNews.* 5 June 2015.

p. xii Number of summons sent. Moore, Thad, Avery Wilks, and Jocelyn Grzeszczak. "Jury Selection in Alex Murdaugh Double Murder Trial Trudges into the Second Day." *Post and Courier.* 23 January 2023.

Introduction

p. 1 Chapter title inspired by a song from the musical *Avenue Q*.

p. 1 "*Perry Mason* is the show that launched a thousand shows; every courtroom drama you've ever seen comes from that template." Blumberg, Perri Ormont. "Why HBO's "Perry Mason" Reboot Isn't the Courtroom Drama Fans Expected" *Southern Living.* 8 July 2020.

p. 1 "passive jury" or "human furniture." Marder, Nancy. "Juror Bias, Voir Dire, and the Judge-Jury Relationship." Chicago-Kent Law Review. 90.3 (2015).

p. 2 "a mockumentary that turns an everyday American experience into a hilarious reality TV experiment as it explores the progression of a civil trial in California through the eyes of one juror who does not realize that everyone, except him, is an actor." McClusky, Megan. "Why Jury Duty is the Show You Should Watch Right Now." *Time.* 26 April 2023.

p. 3   Likewise, Judge Patricia Marks....Papke, David. "The Impact of Popular Culture on American Perceptions of the Courts." Indiana Law Journal. 82.5 (2007).

p. 3   Greeks held fast.... "The Jury in the United States and Iowa." *Iowa Judicial Branch.*

p. 5   A Juror's Prayer. Rebein, Paul W. et al. "Jury (Dis)Service: Why People Avoid Jury Duty and What Florida Can do About It." *Nova Law Review*. 28. (2003).

p. 5   What you wear to court. Boniello Kathianne, "The Wackiest Excuses People Use to Get Out of Jury Duty." *New York Post*. 4 January 2015.

p. 6   .....access to childcare. Keller, John. "Confessions of a Juror: How Jury Duty Impacts Americans." *Bar Prep Hero*. 11 Apr. 2021.

p. 7   South Carolina attorney Eric Bland. Miller, Riley. "South Carolina Attorney: It's Very Possible Alex Murdaugh Could Get a Hung Jury at Murder Trial." *WJCL.com*. 23 January 2023.

Foreword

p. 9   Chapter title inspired by Elvis Costello's song "Watching the Detectives."

Chapter 1

p. 15   Chapter title inspired by Elvis Presley's "Return to Sender."

Chapter 2

p. 21   Chapter title inspired by the Olivia Newton-John and John Travolta's song "You're the One that I Want."

p. 23 "by prohibiting…." Wilks, Avery, Thad Moore and Jocelyn Grzeszczak. "Alex Murdaugh Trial Begins with Explosive Opening Statements, Support From Relatives." *Post
and Courier*. 25 January 2023.

Chapter 3

p. 25 Chapter title inspired by Warren Zevron's "Lawyers, Guns,
and Money."

p. 26 "It is your duty…." "Juror Selection Process." *United States
Courts*.

p. 26 While the Sixth guarantees. "4th, 5th, and 6th Amend-
ments." *The Greening Law Group*. 6 February 2023.

p. 27 Abraham Lincoln defended…. Wilks, Avery. Alex Murdaugh's defense attorneys: Who are Dick Harpootlian and
Jim Griffin? *Post and Courier*. 19 January 2023.

p. 29 Perry Mason moment. "Perry Mason Moment." *Wikipedia*, 13 July 2023.

p. 31 Stressing some of them. "FULL INTERVIEW (Part 1):
Murdaugh Murder Investigators Speak Candidly After Trial." ABC News

p. 32 Dick asked Agent Dalila Cirencione. YouTube video. 25
March 2023.

p. 36 Worley also testified. DeWitt, Michael. "Alex Murdaugh
murder trial: Investigators' testimony continues to reveal
vivid evidence." *Greenville News*. 27 January 2023

p. 36 …trial within a trial. Folks, Will. "Murdaugh Murders'
Saga: A Trial Within A Trial." *FitsNews*. 2 February 2023.

p. 38 These tests consistently Ibbetson, Ross. "Alex Murdaugh's Defense Found Focus Group Had 'a Really Hard Time' Believing State's Claim." *Dailymail.* 7 February 2023.

p. 38 "We thought the state did not have…" "Dynasty of Death." *Crime Nation.* S1: E4. 12 March 2024.

p. 38 "Chewbacca Defense" "Chewbacca Defense." *Wikipedia*, 18 November 2022,

p. 39 During Tony's distressing testimony. McKelvey, Gigi. "Alex Murdaugh Trial: Day 14." *Pretty Lies and Alibis.* 9 February 2023.

p. 40 Betty Bowers Quote. Bowers, Betty. *r/ MurdaughFamily-Murders.* Reddit. 15 September 2021.

Chapter 4

p. 41 Chapter title inspired by the song "Till the Law Says Stop" by Johnny Faire.

p. 41 From there, a bevy of men and one woman. "Pursuing Justice Without Fear or Favor." https://scsolicitor14.org/

p. 42 Commenting further on this powerhouse….Wilks, Avery. "Meet Creighton Waters, the Murdaugh prosecutor whose investigations toppled an SC dynasty." *Post and Courier.* 17 December 2022.

p. 44 Judge Gergel. Monk, John and Ted Cliford. "'Disgrace.' Federal Judge Shows No Mercy for Murdaugh's Many Crimes, Betrayals." *The State.* 2 April 2024.

p. 45 Crighton Waters. "Criminal Investigation." *Wikipedia.* 27 August 2024.

p. 46 Of SC vs. Alex Murdaugh. Jabour, Tara. "Attorney General and Prosecutors Discuss Murdaugh Double Murder Trial." *WCIV*. 29 March 2023.

p. 47 Michael Dewitt. Dewitt, Michael. "Alex Murdaugh Murder Trial: Everything You Need to Know Before Tuesday's Proceedings." *Greenville News*. 30 January 2023.

p. 47 Does it literally help. "Part 2: Murdaugh prosecution team shares unique insights (w/ Creighton Waters, John Meadors, et al)." *ABCNews4*. 5 April 2023.

p. 52 Goude, Savanna. Personal Communication. 17 April 2023.

p. 53 Waters's unwavering belief in Goude. "Mock Trial 101: How to Introduce Real Evidence." *Doherty High School Mock Trial.* 20 April 2024.

p. 53 Michael Dewitt comment. Dewitt, Michael. *X.* 14 October 2023.

p. 54 … mechanical witnesses. Folks, Will. "'Murdaugh Murders'" Saga: Prosecution Witnesses to Watch For." *FitsNews*. 27 January 2023.

p. 57 Her insight was eye-opening. Laudenslager, Chase. "State Delivers Closing Argument in Alex Murdaugh Murder Trial." *Count on News 2.* 1 March 2023.

p. 57 Dr. John Matthias. Mathias, John and Lauren Mathias. "Secrets of the Vault: The Real Motives Behind the Murdaugh Murders." *Hidden True Crime*. YouTube. 4 March 2023.

Chapter 5

p. 61 Chapter title inspired by Marvin Gaye's "Can I Get a Witness"

p. 61 Creighton Waters asserted. "Alex Murdaugh lead prosecutor Creighton Waters Looks Back on the Case." *News 19 WLTX*. YouTube. 3 March 2023.

p. 62 Research shows this can be a real problem. Jason Chin & Larysa Workewych. "The CSI Effect." *Markus Dubber*, ed. *Oxford Handbooks Online* (New York: Oxford University Press, 2016).

p. 64 Dr. Kenny Kinsey. Shaw, Amanda and Brookley Cromer "Murdaugh Trial Witness Says Piece of Evidence Was 'Game Changer.'" *Fox Carolina*. YouTube. 18 April 2023.

p. 66 Fiona Guy. Guy, Fiona. "Color Verses Black and White Photographic Evidence in a Murder Trial." *Crime Traveller*. 19 June 2022.

p. 67 At one point she asked. McKelvey, Gigi. "Murdaugh Trial: Day 16." *Pretty Lies and Alibis*. 13 February 2023

p. 68 When evaluating the overall relevance. "Rule 403: Excluding Relevant Evidence for Prejudice, Confusion, Waste of Time, or Other Reasons." *Cornell Law School*.

p. 68 Dr. Riemer. Riemer, Ellen. Personal Communication. 29 August 2023.

p. 69 Richard Pickett. Reynolds, Joshua and Victoria Estrada-Reynolds. "Investigator Beliefs of Homicide Crime Scene Characteristics." *Applied Psychology in Criminal Justice*. 15.1 (2019).

p. 70   Hidden True Crime podcast. Mathias, John and Lauren Mathias. "Murdaugh Family Crimes: Power and Multi-generational Shame." *Hidden True Crime.* YouTube. 17 February 2023.

p. 75   Charlie Condon. "Murdaugh Day 15 - Charlie Condon and Anne Emerson." WCIV | ABC News 4. 10 February 2023.

p. 75   Career Explorer. "Forensic Pathologist Demographics in the United States." *Career Explorer.* 18 July 2024.

p. 78   We don't comply with subpoenas. McKelvey, Gigi. "Murdaugh Trial: Day 20." *Pretty Lies and Alibis.* 17 February 2023

p. 84   John Meadors. Berry, JR. "Meet Bubba, the Family Dog that Helped Convict Alex Murdaugh of Double Murder." *WLTX.* 18 May 2023.

Chapter 6

p. 87   Chapter title is inspired by Genesis's "Land of Confusion."

p. 89   After Annette's heartrending testimony. Grzeszczak, Jocelyn, Avery G. Wilks, and Thad Moore. "Jurors in Alex Murdaugh Double Murder Trial Hear Financial Witnesses Testify." *Post and Courier.* 7 February 2023.

p. 91   The bailiff offered. Cathon, Graham. "Investigators Say They Know Who Made the Bomb Threat During Alex Murdaugh's Murder Trial." *WJCL News 22.* 23 February 2023.

p. 93   We wanted it run and practiced. "Full Interview (Part 2) Murdaugh Murder Investigation." *ABC News 4.* YouTube. 28 March 2023.

p. 94   Liz Farrel. Farrel, Liz. Tweet. 22 February 2023.

Chapter 7

p. 97   Chapter title is inspired by The Animals's "House of the Rising Sun."

p. 98   Natalie Gordon. Moorhouse, Drusilla. "Juries Visited the Crime Scenes in These Five Murder Trials. Here's Why That Can't Happen in the Idaho Stabbings Case." *Buzzfeed News.* 21 March 2023.

p. 98   Bauerlein, Valerie. "Pool Reporter Notes." 1 March 2023.

p. 101   Melendez, Pilar. "How Alex Murdaugh's Murder Trial Was Almost Derailed by a Bomb Threat." *The Daily Beast.* 13 August 2023.

p. 102   At extremely close range. "Jurors in Alex Murdaugh's murder trial travel to Moselle, site of the Slayings." *Post and Courier: Understand Murdaugh.* 1 March 2023. S1E42.

p. 105   The Daily Mail. Ibbetson, Ross. "Jury are Escorted to Family's Moselle Hunting Lodge." *Dailymail 1* March 2023.

p. 107   She told attorney Meadors…. Ortiz, Erik. "Murdaugh Family Housekeeper Testifies that Alex's Wife said He 'Was Not Being Truthful.'" *NBC News.* 10 February 2023.

p. 108   Conspicuously placed. Burrough, Nicholas. "Jurors in Murdaugh Murder Trial Visit S.C. Crime Scene." *New York Times*. 1 March 2023

p. 108   O.J. Simpson would. O'Keeffe, Jack. "American Crime Story' Shows A Big Home Makeover.' *Bustle.* 1 March 2016.

Chapter 8

p. 109 Chapter title is inspired by Isaac Hayes's "I Stand Accused."

p. 109 The phrase is typically... Temme, Laura. "Fifth Amendment Grand Jury, Self-Incrimination, and Due Process Protections." *Find Law*. 15 February 2022.

p. 109 Lithwick, Dahlia. "Where Did the Fifth Amendment Come From." *Slate*. 12 February 2002.

p. 110 ...then just hope the jury..... Davies, Wade. "Should the Defendant Testify?" Tennessee Bar Association Law Blog. 1 March 2018. Vol. 54 No.

p. 110 Peter Schorsch. Schorsch, Peter. "Charlie Adelson Trial Recap: An 'absurd' Defense." *Florida Politics* 6 November 2023

p. 111 ....many small things.... Keane, Isabel. "Jennifer Crumbley Juror Reveals Verdict Was Not Initially Unanimous." *New York Post*. 7 February 2024.

p. 111 ....which may be misconstrued for guilt. Elmen, Robert. "Should You Testify in Your Criminal Case." *Criminal Lawyers of Ann Arbor*. 27 December 2023.

p. 113 After all, that single piece..... Pines, Noah. "Lalibi." *Opening Statements with Julie Grant*.

p. 114 He maintained eye......McKelvey, Gigi. "Alex Murdaugh Trial: Day 23." *Pretty Lies and Alibis*.

p. 119 He was answering...... "Analysis with Trial Attorney Carl B. Grant of the Alex Murdaugh Murder Trial." *WIS*. 23 February 2023.

p. 120 There are so many things….Chappell, Bill and Victoria Hansen. "Here are 8 Big Revelations from the Alex Murdaugh Murder Trial." *NPR*. 3 March 2023.

p. 121 They will have to decide….. "As Murdaugh Trial Winds Down, Will Jury Believe He Distrusted Police?" *Crime and Justice News*

p. 121 Substack writer Anne Fernandez. Fernandez, Anne. "The Anxiety of Alex Murdaugh." *Substack.* 26 February 2023.

p. 124 In doing this….Driver, Janine. "Body Language Expert Weighs in on Alex Murdaugh Testimony." *CNN* YouTube. 24 February 2023

p. 124 Further saying….Glass, Lillian. "Alex Murdaugh's Body Language 'Doesn't Lie.'" *News Nation*. YouTube. 24 February 2023.

p. 125 When discussing checking Paul….Garris, John. "Psychologist and Body Language Expert Exposes Alex Murdaugh's Hidden Behaviors." *Dr. G Explains*. YouTube. 9 March 2023.

p. 125 We saw that…..Driver, Janine. "Psychologist and Body Language Expert Exposes Alex Murdaugh's Hidden Behaviors." *Court TV* 25 February 2023.

Chapter 9

p. 129 Chapter title inspired by Pigmeat Markham's "Here Comes the Judge."

p. 130 Elaborating further… "Member Spotlight with Judge Clifton Newman." *American Bar Association*. 28 September 2017.

p. 130   In a commencement address…..."Judge Clifton Newman Delivers Keynote and Receives Honorary Degree." *Post and Courier.* 24 May 2024

p. 131   We carry the weight….Helling, Steve. "What to know about South Carolina Judge Who Sentenced Alex Murdaugh" *People.com* 2 March 2023.

p. 132   Hawes, Jennifer Berry. "Murdaugh Cases Overseen by SC Judge Clifton Newman." *Post and Courier.* 2 September 2022.

p. 132   Kevin Fisher. "Here's to the Judge, the Jury and John Meadors." *Post and Courier* 12 March 2023

p. 132   Jared Newman. Shore, Jake. "SC Supreme Court Assigns Outside Judge to Oversee Alex Murdaugh Criminal Cases." *Island Packet.* 3 June 2023

p. 132   John Meadors. Mark, Michelle and Ashley Collman. "Trial Judge Showed Quiet Restraint Until it was Time for Sentencing." *Business Insider.* 4 March 2023

p. 141   The defense counsel…. Farrell, Liz. "One Picture, So Many Different Images." *The Island News.* 22 February 2023.

p. 142   …"told her podcast audience." Baker, Emily. *Emily D. Baker.* YouTube. 24 January 2023.

p. 143   For example, when…..Ibbetson, Ross. "Buster Murdaugh Accused of Flipping the Bird at a Witness." *Daily Mail. com* 9 February 2023.

p. 143   Lynne – like Buster…..Sharp, Rachel. "Alex Murdaugh Family Warned They Will Be Thrown Out of Murder Trial." *The Independent.* 10 February 2023.

p. 143 In an earlier, chapter….Sokol, Matthew. "Alex Murdaugh Charged with New Misdemeanor." *ABC News 4*. 27 February 2023.

p. 146 In April…Dewitt, Michael. "Murdaugh Murder Trial Judge Clifton Newman Takes Major step in Legal Career." *Greeneville News*. 5 April 2024.

Chapter 10

p. 147 Chapter title is inspired by a song from the musical *Hamilton*.

p. 148 Then time suddenly…"Veridct." *CourtTV.*

p. 156 It was reported…. Wright, Bailey. "Jury in Murdaugh Murder Trial Reaches Verdict." *ABC News 4*. 2 March 2023.

Chapter 11

p. 161 Chapter title inspired by Stevie Wonders's song "Signed Sealed Delivered."

p. 163 McKelvey, Gigi. "Murdaugh Trial: Day 28." *Pretty Lies and Alibis*. 2 March 2023.

p. 167 This movement…. Driver, Janine. "Analyzing Alex Murdaugh's Body Language During Verdict and Sentencing." Court TV. 3 March 2023.

p. 168 Shortly after the verdict….Glass, Lillian. "What did Murdaugh's Body Language Say When He Heard the Guilty Verdict? | Morning in America." *News Nation*. 2 March 2023.

p. 170 Banfield, Ashely. "'Shocked' by Alex Murdaugh verdict | On Balance." *News Nation*. YouTube. 2 March 2023.

p. 171 Abrams, Dan. "Murdaugh Verdict: Reaction to Timing of Jury Deliberations Mixed | Dan Abrams Live." *News Nation*. YouTube. 2 March 2023.

p. 172 Grant, Carl. "Alex Murdaugh murder trial verdict analysis." *WIS*. YouTube. 2 March 2023.

p. 175 Newman, Clifton. "Judge Clifton Newman on Alex Murdaugh Verdict." *Today*. 21 June 2023.

Chapter 12

p. 183 Chapter title inspired by Merle Haggard's "Life in Prison."

p. 186 For almost 20 minutes. Fava. Mark. "Aviator Lawyer Lady Justice and Judge Newman." 16 April 2023

p. 186 In addition, there is…."Alex Murdaugh Officially in Prison to Begin Serving Life Sentence." *WLTX*. YouTube. 3 March 2023.

Epilogue

p. 189 Chapter title is inspired by Soul II Soul's "Back to Life Back to Reality."

Preface II

p. 195 Chapter title is inspired by Kitty Wells's song "Will Your Lawyer Talk to God."

Chapter 1

p. 199 Chapter title inspired by 10,000 Maniacs's "What's the Matter Here."

p. 200 "…there are serious…" Dewitt, Michael. "Murdaugh lawyers demand new trial, FBI investigation, Accuse Clerk Becky Hill of Jury Tampering." *Greenville News*. 5 September 2023.

Chapter 2

p. 203 Chapter title was inspired by Bonnie Raitt's song "Something to Talk About."

p. 205 They told the world…. Dewitt, Michael. "Murdaugh Trial Jury Tampering Allegations: SLED Investigating, Familiar Attorneys Involved." *Greenville News*. 8 September 2023.

Chapter 3

p. 215 Title inspired by Chuck Brodsky's "Talk to My Lawyer."

p. 219 We believe…..McDougall, AJ. "Alex Murdaugh Loses Prison Privileges Over Recorded Call for Fox Documentary." *Daily Beast*. 30 August 2023.

p. 219 "Newman had made…" Monk, John and Ted Clifford. "Murdaugh's Lawyers ask SC Supreme Court to Kick Judge Newman Off the case." *The State*. 2 November 2023.

p. 222 I think she will recognize. Monk, John. "Former SC Chief Justice Jean Toal Appointed to Oversee all Murdaugh Murder Appeal Issues. *The State*. 20 December 2023.

p. 222 Dayne Phillips. Lawson, Walker. "Former SC Chief Justice Takes Charge of High-Profile Murder Conviction Case." *WLTX*. 20 December 2023.

Chapter 4

p. 225 Chapter title inspired by Roger and Hammerstein's "I'm Gonna Wash That Man Right Outta My Hair."

p. 227 Now almost 20 percent. "Chief Justice Jean Toal." *South Carolina Judicial Branch. sccourts.org*

p. 227 They worked on strategy and briefs…. "Jean Hoeffer Toal." *Columbia City of Women*. 15 August 2024.

p. 227 …To me…. Marchant, Bristow. "Becky Hill Heard 'Siren Call of Celebrity,' SC Judge Says in Murdaugh Case." *The State*. 29 January 2024.

p. 234 When Meadors…… Emerson, Anne et. al. "Judge Denies Murdaugh's Motion for Retrial in Monday's Jury Tampering Hearing." *ABC NEWS 4*. 29 January 2024.

Epilogue

p. 237 Chapter title inspired by Cage the Elephant's song "No Rest for the Wicked."

Afterword

p. 247 Chapter title inspired by Snoop Dog's "Murder was the Case."

ADDITIONAL WORKS CONSULTED

"Brilliant Strategy to Have Murdaugh Testify." Cuomo. 23 February 2023.

Brown, Martha. "Orangeburg's Kinsey Star Witness at Murdaugh Trial." *The Times and Democrat*. 11 March 2023.

Collins, Jeffrey. "Brutality Detailed in Alex Murdaugh Case; 2 Jurors Get Covid." *Fox5*. 13 February 2023.

Dewitt, Michael, Jr. "Alex Murdaugh Trial Updates: Autopsy Report Reveals Chilling Manner Murdaughs Were Murdered." *Greenville News*. 13 February 2023,

Kalmbacher, Colin. "Alex Murdaugh Murder Trial Begins with Opening Statements After Jury is Seated." *Law and Crime*. 25 July 2023.

Laudenslager, Chase and Riley Benson. "Prosecutor John Meadors Speaks for the First Time since Murdaugh Murder Trial." *Post and Courier*. 9 Mar 2023.

Mack, David. "How an Unruly Labrador Retriever and a 50-Second Video Led to Alex Murdaugh's Downfall." *Buzzfeed*. 2 March 2023.

Papke, David Ray. "'12 Angry Men' Is Not an Archetype: Reflections on the Jury

Contemporary Popular Culture." Chicago-Kent Law Review. 82.2 (2007).

Phang, Katie. "Netflix's Latest Villain Alex Murdaugh Did Not Help Himself by Testifying." MSNBC Opinion. 27 February 2023.

Rathe, Adam. "Perry Mason was the Original Law and Order." 5 July 2020. Town and Country.

Slater, Dashika. "Court Potato." Legal Affairs. May/June

Stryker, Timothy. "Alex Murdaugh's 911 Call." Malke Crime Notes. 28 July 2022,

"Three Type of Witness Testimony in a Criminal Case." Keller Law Offices: Criminal Defense and Trial Attorneys. 20 February 2020.

Tripp, Drew and Baily Wright. "Murdaugh Trial Day 17 Witnesses: Maggie's Sister, Forensic Pathologist and Kennel Caretaker." Abc15News. 14 February 2023.

Printed in the USA
CPSIA information can be obtained
at www.ICGtesting.com
LVHW052019061224
798426LV00021B/677

* 9 7 9 8 8 2 2 9 5 4 2 2 9 *